PET Result

Student's Book

Jenny Quintana

OXFORD
UNIVERSITY PRESS

Contents

		Reading	Writing
1	**Holidays and travel** page 18	Part 3 True / False	Part 2 A postcard
2	**Learning** page 24	Part 2 Matching	Part 3 An informal letter
3	**Buying and selling** page 30	Part 1 Multiple choice Part 5 Multiple-choice cloze	Part 1 Sentence transformations Part 2 An email
4	**Animals and humans** page 38	Part 4 Multiple choice	Part 3 An informal letter
5	**Health and sport** page 44	Part 3 True / False	Part 2 An email
6	**Homes and lifestyles** page 50	Part 2 Matching	A short advert Part 3 An informal letter
7	**Art and entertainment** page 58	Part 4 Multiple choice	Part 2 An email
8	**Safety** page 64	Part 1 Multiple choice	Part 3 A story
9	**Science and technology** page 70	Part 3 True / False	Part 3 An informal letter
10	**Relationships** page 76	Part 2 Matching	Part 3 A story
11	**The natural world** page 84	Part 4 Multiple choice	Part 3 An informal letter
12	**Food and celebrations** page 90	Part 1 Multiple choice	Part 3 A story
13	**TV and media** page 96	Part 4 Multiple choice	Part 2 An email
14	**Communicating** page 102	Part 1 Multiple choice Part 5 Multiple-choice cloze	Part 3 A story

Introductory Unit page 8–17

Review 1 page 36–37

Review 2 page 56–57

Review 3 page 82–83

Review 4 page 108–109

Listening	Speaking	Grammar	Vocabulary
Part 2 Multiple choice Part 1 Multiple choice	Holidays	The past simple and past continuous	Travel and transport Holidays Countryside
Part 4 True / false	Parts 3 and 4	Adverbs of frequency The present simple and present continuous	Hobbies and leisure *make, do, have, take* Education
Part 2 Multiple choice	Shopping Part 2	Countable and uncountable nouns Quantity	Shopping Clothes and accessories
Part 3 Gapfill	Part 3 Films	Comparative and superlative adjectives	Animals Parts of the body Films
Part 2 Multiple choice	Sport Part 2	The present perfect The present perfect with *for* and *since*	Health, medicine and exercise Sport
Part 3 Gapfill	Parts 1, 3 and 4	The past perfect	House and home Adjectives
Part 4 True / False Part 1 Multiple choice	Part 3	Order of adjectives Gerunds and infinitives	Entertainment
Part 3 Gapfill	Part 2	Obligation, prohibition and necessity Ability and possibility	Household objects Weather
Part 4 True / False	Parts 3 and 4	The passive Agreeing and disagreeing	Technology Work and jobs
Part 1 Multiple choice	Part 2	Possessive forms The future	Family Personality adjectives Phrasal verbs with *get*
Part 2 Multiple choice	Parts 3 and 4	Zero and first conditional Second conditional Sentence transformations	The natural world Verbs and prepositions Phrasal verbs
Part 4 True / False	Food Part 2	Comparative and superlative adverbs Reported speech Sentence transformations	Food and drink Celebrations
Part 1 Multiple choice	Part 1 Free time	*used to*	Entertainment and media
Part 3 Gapfill	Interviews Parts 3 and 4	*have something done* Sentence transformations Expressing purpose	Personal feelings

Exam Overview	**Writing Guide**	**Vocabulary Reference**	**Grammar Reference**
page 4–7	page 110–112	page 113–117	page 118–127

Exam Overview

Introduction

The Preliminary English Test corresponds to Level Two in the Cambridge ESOL five-level system. It also corresponds to the Association of Language Teachers in Europe (ALTE) Level Two, and Council of Europe level B1.

There are three papers in the examination: Reading and Writing, Listening, and Speaking. To get a passing grade, candidates must achieve 70% of the total marks available, or above. Candidates are graded on the total score from all three papers and there is no pass or fail grade for individual papers.

Paper 1 Reading and Writing (1 hour 30 minutes)

Reading

The Reading Paper has five parts and 35 questions. The reading texts are short texts such as notices, signs, messages, emails and labels, and longer, adapted texts.

Part	Number of items	Task type	What you do	What it tests	How to do it
1	5	Three-option multiple-choice	Read short notices or messages for the main message.	Your understanding of everyday notices and other short texts.	page 31
2	5	Matching	Read short texts and match with descriptions of people.	Your detailed comprehension of different texts.	page 52
3	10	True / False	Answer true / false questions about a longer factual text.	Your ability to find specific information while ignoring unimportant material.	page 18
4	5	Four-option multiple choice	Answer four-option multiple-choice questions on a longer attitude or opinion text.	Your ability to understand both the whole picture and the details and to understand the writer's attitude, opinion and purpose for writing.	page 59
5	10	Four-option multiple-choice cloze	Complete a short passage, which can be factual or narrative.	Your understanding of vocabulary and grammar in a short text.	page 105

Marks

25% of total marks for the whole examination.

Writing

The Writing Paper has three parts and seven questions.

Part 1 tests common grammatical structures. You read a sentence, then complete a gapped sentence so that it means the same as the first sentence. You will need to write between one and three words to fill the gap. Answers of more than three words will be marked wrong, and spelling must be correct.

In Part 2 you are told who to write to and why, and must include the three points given in the question.

In Part 3 you choose to write either a story or an informal letter. For the story you are given the title or the first sentence. For the informal letter you read an extract from a letter and are told what to write in response.

Part	Number of items	Task type	What you do	What it tests	How to do it
1	5	Sentence transformations	Change the grammatical structure or vocabulary of a sentence but keep the same meaning.	Your knowledge of grammatical structures.	page 86
2	1	Short communicative message	Write a postcard, note or email of about 35–45 words.	Effective communication of key information.	page 23
3	1	Longer piece of continuous writing	Write a longer piece of about 100 words from a choice of two questions, an informal letter or a story.	Organisation, spelling, punctuation, accuracy and range of language.	page 69

Marks

25% of total marks for the whole examination.

Exam Overview

Paper 2 Listening (approximately 30 minutes)

The Listening Paper has four parts and 25 questions. All parts are heard twice. The instructions are given on the question paper and are also heard. The recordings include a variety of voices, styles of delivery and accents.

Part	Number of items	Task type	What you do	What it tests	How to do it
1	7	Multiple choice	Answer questions on short monologues or dialogues.	Your ability to identify important information from short texts.	page 80
2	6	Multiple choice	Answer questions on a longer monologue or interview.	Your ability to identify detailed information in longer recordings.	page 46
3	6	Gap-fill	Complete notes based on a longer monologue.	Your ability to listen to, identify, understand and interpret information.	page 51
4	6	True / False	Answer true / false questions about a longer dialogue.	Your ability to listen for detailed meaning, and to identify the attitudes and opinions of the speakers.	page 60

Marks

25% of total marks for the whole examination.

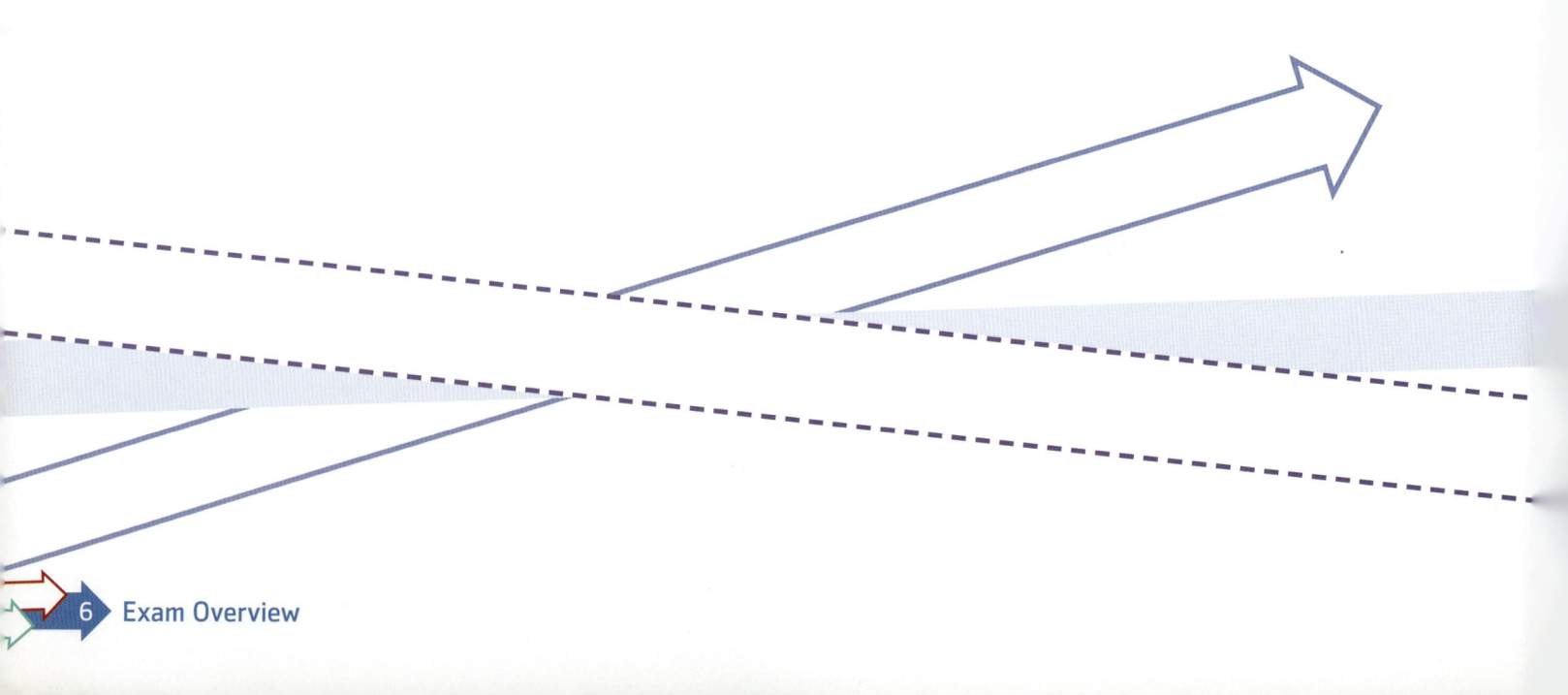

Exam Overview

Paper 3 Speaking (10–12 minutes)

The Speaking Paper has four parts. There are two candidates and two examiners. One examiner (the interlocutor) will ask the candidates questions and the other (the assessor) just listens. If there is an uneven number of candidates, three candidates may sit the test together and the test will take slightly longer.

Part	Length	Task type	What you do	What it tests	How to do it
1	2–3 minutes	A conversation between the interlocutor and each candidate.	Answer questions about yourself, your past experiences and plans.	Your ability to give information of a factual, personal kind.	page 54
2	2–3 minutes	A simulated situation which candidates do together.	Discuss a task based on pictures.	Your ability to use language to make and respond to suggestions, discuss alternatives, make recommendations and to agree and disagree.	page 77
3	3 minutes	An extended turn for each candidate.	Talk about a photograph for approximately one minute.	Your ability to describe a photograph and use appropriate vocabulary in a longer turn.	page 61
4	3 minutes	A general conversation between the candidates.	Discuss topics related to the photographs.	Your ability to talk about likes and dislikes, opinions, preferences, experiences and habits.	page 74

Marks

Candidates are assessed on their performance throughout the test. There are 25 marks which make up 25% of the total score for the whole examination.

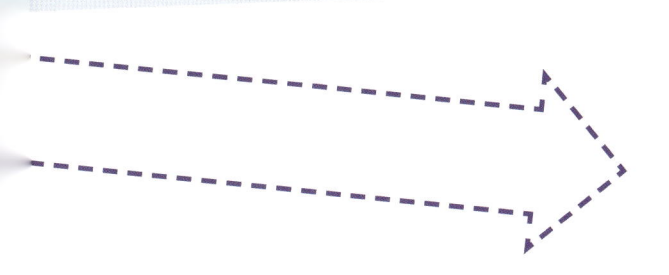

Introductory Unit

Reading 1

1 Look at texts 1–6 and match them with text types a–c.
   a text message   c postcard
   b notice

> **1** Why don't we meet up on Friday and play tennis? Please let me know before 5.30 because I need to book the court today.

> **2** ANY BIKES LEFT HERE WILL BE REMOVED IMMEDIATELY

> **3** It's a beautiful place – the beach is fantastic and within easy walking distance of the hotel. The weather's great too! Wish you were here with us!

> **4** Identity cards must be shown in order to enter building

> **5** We have to be at the sports centre before 9 tomorrow morning. Shall I meet you at the corner of Green Street so we can walk there together?

> **6** USE OF MOBILE PHONES FORBIDDEN INSIDE HOSPITAL

2 Match these phrases from the texts in exercise 1 with purposes a–f below.
   1 why don't we meet up
   2 please let me know
   3 bikes left here will be removed
   4 identity cards must be shown
   5 we have to be at the sports centre
   6 use of mobiles forbidden

   a a prohibition / something not allowed
   b a rule
   c a suggestion
   d a polite request
   e a warning
   f an obligation

3 Put these phrases into three groups of similar meanings.
   a it is prohibited   f it is forbidden
   b it is required   g you can
   c it is permitted   h it is necessary
   d it is allowed   i it is not allowed
   e you need to   j you mustn't

4 Using the phrases from exercise 3, discuss some rules for your school or where you work.

5 Read messages 1 and 2 and decide what they mean (A, B or C).

> **1** Hi Elena I think I left my wallet on your kitchen table. Please check for me and see if there are two theatre tickets inside. I'll need them on Saturday night. Give me a ring as soon as possible! Love Joanna.

   A Joanna wants Elena to confirm that the theatre tickets in her wallet are safe.
   B Joanna wants Elena to check she has theatre tickets for the right evening.
   C Joanna wants Elena to call her about the wallet she lost in the theatre.

Hi Martin

I've just heard that my science project must be completed before Friday and not next week! Can you come round and help me finish it tonight?

Eduardo

A Eduardo wants Martin to help him with his project next week.
B Eduardo tells Martin to finish his project on Friday if possible.
C Eduardo needs Martin's help so he can finish his project quickly.

6 Read texts 1–3 and match them with photos A–C. What can you learn on each course?

1 If you have a sense of adventure, come to Kenya, where you'll be able to learn to take dramatic and unusual photographs of wildlife! The course will be taught by the famous photographer David Gilbert. Ideally, you will have previous experience of photography. This is a demanding trip – you will need to be up early each day to get the best opportunities, but if you are patient, you could get that perfect picture!

2 Learn to paint in one of the most beautiful parts of Italy and stay in a historic village with fantastic views of the surrounding countryside. No previous experience of painting is necessary and you will get a lot of encouragement from your tutors. You will also get the chance to visit some of the best restaurants, serving a range of delicious local dishes. Day trips to nearby places of historic interest are available but not included in the price.

3 If you love dancing and already do it regularly but want to improve your skills, this is the course for you. Courses in the exciting city of Seville in Spain range from just three days to a fortnight. With four hours of classes a day, you need to be fit and full of energy, but there is also plenty of time to go shopping and sightseeing. As well as learning to dance, there is an optional conversation class to improve your language skills!

7 For texts 1–3 in exercise 6, make as many sentences as you can beginning in these ways:
- On this course you can …
- On this course you must …
- On this course you might …
- On this course you should …

8 Read texts 1–3 again, and match each one with these people. Underline the parts of the text which give you the answers.
  a Peter is a very active and sporty person.
  b Sue is a keen cook and loves eating out.
  c Tim has always been interested in animals.
  d Isabel would like some tips to improve her skills with a camera.
  e Mark would love to be an artist but has never had any lessons.
  f Wendy speaks a little Spanish but would like to be more fluent.

9 Discuss these questions with a partner.
  a Would you like to go on any of the holidays in exercise 6? Why / Why not?
  b What sort of holiday would you like to go on where you could learn something?

Introductory Unit 9

Writing

1 All of these sentences contain a mistake with spelling or grammar. Write S for spelling or G for grammar and correct the mistake.

   a I recieved a nice present from my friend.
   b When I will get home, I will call you.
   c I hope to see you tomorow!
   d He asked me how old am I.
   e I like all types of music especialy rock.
   f I must to do my homework before I go out.
   g The football match last night was very exiting.
   h Yesterday I have been to London.
   i Where you went last night?
   j This car is more cheap than all the others.
   k I don't think there is nobody in the house.

2 Sentences a–h each contain at least one punctuation mistake. Find and correct it.

   a I study english and german.
   b My sisters got three mobiles.
   c I'm going to london. Because there are many interesting places to see.
   d I like football rugby and athletics.
   e How old are you.
   f This book, which he wrote ten year's ago is still very popular.
   g Shes coming to see me later this morning.
   h My friend doesnt have time to do his homework.

> **tip** Always check your work for mistakes with spelling, grammar and punctuation.

3 Put adverbs a–i into four groups with similar meanings.

   a in fact
   b fortunately
   c obviously
   d surprisingly
   e actually
   f naturally
   g of course
   h luckily
   i to my surprise

4 Complete these sentences using an appropriate word or phrase from exercise 3.

   a It started to rain but .... I had my umbrella with me.
   b She didn't receive a birthday card from her best friend so .... she felt very disappointed.
   c I got up early this morning. .... I got up before six!
   d He studied all day but .... he wasn't tired at all!
   e She passed all her exams so .... she was very happy.

5 Read the story and complete gaps 1–6 with six of these words. There may be more than one possible answer.

but	when	although	so
because	despite	then	while

(1).................. I woke up late, I was able to catch the 8 am bus. I arrived at the railway station and was very happy (2).................. there wasn't a queue in the ticket office. I had a little time before my train arrived (3).................. I went to buy a coffee. (4).................. I got there I was surprised to see an old friend I hadn't seen for many years. We started to chat and (5).................. I forgot the time! Suddenly I noticed my train arriving at the platform. (6).................. running as fast as I could, I missed the train.

Introductory Unit

6 Look at the example, then rewrite each of a–e in two different ways, using the linking words from exercise 5.

Example he was late for work / his boss didn't get angry
He was late for work but his boss didn't get angry.
Although he was late for work, his boss didn't get angry.

a I felt very tired / I went to bed early
b I got home / I had a shower
c it was dark / I couldn't see anything
d Pablo works hard / he never seems tired
e Emma won the prize / she was congratulated by her teacher

7 Put these adjectives into pairs of similar meanings.

a frightened
b amazed
c angry
d annoyed
e surprised
f happy
g sad
h disappointed
i scared
j pleased

tip Your writing will be more interesting if you use a range of vocabulary.

8 Complete these sentences with your own ideas and then talk about them in pairs.

a The last time I was really disappointed was when …
b I get annoyed when …
c My favourite films are ones that make me feel …
d I will be surprised if …
e I would be very excited if ….

9 Look at these titles. Decide which is the best one for the story in exercise 5.

a A day that started badly
b A big surprise
c A celebration
d A journey I will never forget
e The day I won a prize
f My last day at school

10 Which of the adjectives from exercise 7 are you most likely to use in the stories in exercise 9?

Introductory Unit 11

Reading 2

1 Read this text. What is Stagecoach?

Stagecoach Theatre Arts is a national network of part-time theatre schools for children aged 4 to 16. It was started in 1988 and currently has over 600 centres throughout the UK and a further 50 overseas.

05 Stagecoach offers young people a basic training in the performance skills of drama, dance and singing, which helps build their confidence and develop their character and ability to communicate with others. We limit class sizes to 15, and the courses run for three hours at weekends with shorter sessions for
10 the younger children.

Although Stagecoach is open to all young people with an interest in acting and singing, it provides opportunities for the most talented to perform professionally, and some of
15 our students have been successful in film, television and on the stage.

2 Read sentences a–f. Find words or phrases in the text above with a similar meaning to the underlined information.
   a Stagecoach <u>began</u> in 1988.
   b <u>Today</u> it has over 600 centres.
   c There are 50 centres <u>in other countries</u>.
   d We <u>have a maximum of</u> 15 students in each class.
   e Stagecoach gives young people <u>a chance</u> to become famous.
   f Some students have become stars <u>in the theatre</u>.

3 Read the text opposite about Martin Kim, a young pianist who gives concerts all over the world. Then complete sentences a–f with a suitable word or phrase.
   a Martin's father .... him to become a pianist.
   b It was .... for Martin to learn to play the piano.
   c At school, Martin's exam results were very ....
   d Martin didn't .... the same activities as his friends.
   e At his first public concert, Martin was too nervous to .... himself.
   f Martin thinks children could .... a lot from him about playing the piano.

Introductory Unit

I was born into a musical family. Both my parents were talented musicians so I guess there was always a good chance I would become a musician too!
05 My father actually wasn't keen on the idea of me taking up his career; in his view it wasn't suitable for me.

I actually started playing when I was four. It came naturally to me. However,
10 at school I thought of becoming a doctor because I was doing so well in my exams. In my opinion, if you are getting good grades people expect you to follow a serious career like
15 medicine.

I was sometimes a bit lonely as a child and the friends I had didn't always understand why I wanted to stay inside and practise on the piano, even
20 in the middle of the summer. They wanted me to play football with them.

My first public concert was in my hometown five years ago. The first time I performed I felt extremely
25 nervous – too nervous to have a good time. I suppose my first few concerts were not that good, though everyone was very kind. Now I really enjoy being on the stage.

30 One day I'd love to teach children how to play the piano. I believe I might be quite good at doing that. I want others to experience some of the passion and joy I feel about music.

4 Read the text again and decide if these sentences about Martin are true (T) or false (F).
   a He is surprised that he became a musician.
   b He wasn't good enough to become a doctor.
   c He only played football during the summer.
   d He thinks his first concerts were his best ones.

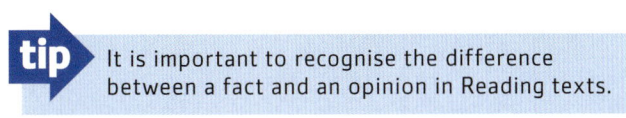

> **tip** It is important to recognise the difference between a fact and an opinion in Reading texts.

5 Underline at least four phrases in the text which express an opinion.

Introductory Unit

Listening

1 Look at pictures 1–3 and say what the differences are between them.

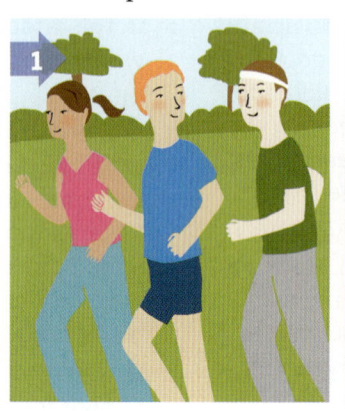

2 Match the pictures in exercise 1 with these descriptions.
A There was a great atmosphere at the football match!
B I really thought I had a chance of winning the race.
C I enjoy keeping fit by jogging in the park with friends.

3 ▶1 Listen to the conversation. Which picture in exercise 1 shows how John is planning to spend his weekends?

4 ▶2 Listen to sentences a–g and circle the number you hear.

a 6.15   5.45
b 16,337   16,733
c 1814   1840
d 18   80
e 15.45   15.55
f 13.5   135.5
g 7th   17th

5 ▶3 Listen to the conversation and complete the table with the missing words. Make sure your spelling is correct.

1	name of the city	....
2	name of the street	.... Street
3	an interesting section visitors should see	the .... section
4	name of the museum director	Mrs ....
5	name of the new gallery	The .... Gallery
6	you can see paintings by	John ....

tip In Listening Part 3 you must spell words correctly.

Introductory Unit

6 Match phrases a–g with similar meanings in 1–7.

a I was disappointed.
b I'm looking forward to it.
c I doubt it.
d It was brilliant.
e I don't feel like it.
f I'm not very keen on it.
g It's a waste of time.

1 I don't want to do it.
2 I loved it.
3 I thought it would be better.
4 It's pointless.
5 It's unlikely.
6 I can't wait!
7 I don't really like it.

7 ▶4 Listen to five sentences and decide which option, a or b, has a similar meaning to what you hear.

1 a He liked the concert.
　b He didn't like the concert.

2 a She is happy with the price.
　b She is unhappy with the price.

3 a He is happy with his team.
　b He is not happy with his team.

4 a She was surprised by what she saw.
　b She was not surprised by what she saw.

5 a He would prefer to go swimming.
　b He would prefer to go riding.

8 ▶5 Listen to two people talking about their local park. Decide if sentences a–h are correct or incorrect.

a Anna prefers the park when it is busy.
b They had to pay for the concert in the park.
c Tom enjoyed the concert.
d Anna liked the singer.
e Anna thinks that there will be less litter in the park next time.
f They both love the park.
g Anna thinks Clara will accept their invitation.
h Tom is looking forward to going to the park.

Introductory Unit

Speaking

1 Read this text then complete a–e with the correct tenses or verb forms. Use a different one each time.

I like holidays by the sea but I don't enjoy spending time in museums. Last year my family and I went to Greece and I spent most of the week on the beach. Next month we are going to Florida. I've been to Canada, but I've never been to the United States, so I'm really looking forward to it. I'd like to go to Disneyland, but I don't know whether there will be enough time.

a talking about habits and facts   *present simple*
b talking about past events   ....
c talking about experiences   ....
d talking about plans for the future   ....
e talking about things you want to do   ....

2 In pairs, talk about a–e, using appropriate tenses.

a what you usually do in your free time   d your holiday experiences
b your plans for next year   e places you'd like to visit in the future
c what you did last summer

3 Match a–j with photo 1 or 2 below.

a salad   c feed   e juice   g restaurant   i jeans
b park   d picnic   f carry   h basket   j baby

4 In pairs, each choose one of the photos and tell your partner about it. Use these ideas to help you.

- How many people are there in the photos? Who are they?
- Where are they?
- What are they doing?
- What are they wearing?
- How do you think they are they feeling?
- Do you enjoy doing the same things? Why / Why not?

16 Introductory Unit

5 Read the conversation between Christina and Maria. In each of 1–4 use one word to complete their suggestions.

Christina   It's grandma's birthday tomorrow. I really don't know what to get her. What do you think?
Maria   Well, we (1)................. get her some chocolates.
Christina   No, that's not a good idea. We always give her chocolates!
Maria   That's true. (2)................. don't we buy her that lovely scarf we saw the other day? I think it would really suit her! How about you?
Christina   I'm sorry but I don't agree, Maria. It's not the right colour for her. She'd prefer something brighter.
Maria   Didn't she say she'd like some new CDs?
Christina   I don't think so. It was mum who said that. How (3)................. some flowers? I'm sure she'd like them.
Maria   Yes, you're right! And we don't usually get flowers, do we? (4)................. we go to the shop and get them now?

6 Read the conversation in exercise 5 again and underline
  a two phrases asking for an opinion
  b two phrases showing agreement
  c three phrases showing disagreement

7 Imagine you are going camping for the weekend. Look at the pictures and do the following in pairs. Use the phrases in exercise 5 to help you.
  a name the objects shown
  b discuss why each one might be useful
  c decide which one would be the best object to take with you

Introductory Unit

1 Holidays and travel

Lead in VR p113

Look at photos A–C of different holidays. Discuss these questions.

a Which is most similar to the holidays you usually go on? How?
b Which looks most enjoyable? Why?

Reading Part 3

1 Read the extract from a holiday brochure on page 19 and say what each photo A–D shows.

2 Read the **how to do it** box, then decide if sentences 1–10 are correct or incorrect.

> **how to do it**
> Read the title and text quickly for general meaning.
> Don't worry about any difficult words, they may not be important.
> Read the sentences and underline the key words.
> Read the text again carefully and decide whether each sentence is correct or incorrect.

1 There are activities for teenagers on both sea and land.
2 These holidays are for teenagers and their families.
3 There are opportunities to learn a sport in northern Thailand.
4 On their last evening in the north, the teenagers cook for local people.
5 Diving to see the sharks is early in the day.
6 On the organised dive, some of the sharks are dangerous.
7 Day two of the visit to Phuket involves exploring the island on foot.
8 Accommodation on Days 8 and 9 is in two different types of hotel.
9 The trip offers sightseeing and shopping trips in Bangkok.
10 All the teenagers most enjoyed seeing the animals.

3 Would you like to go on a trip like this? Why / Why not?

18 Unit 1

A VISIT TO THAILAND

Thailand is a great place for teenagers looking for adventure. Along the coast, you'll find magnificent beaches, the world's bluest waters, and some of the best diving. On land, look out for temples, explore ancient ruins, visit elephant and tiger rescue projects and try delicious food. Our tours are specially designed for teenagers who are going on holiday alone, perhaps for the first time. Here is what you can expect ...

DAYS 1–5

After you land in Bangkok, you fly to the north of the country. Here, you can learn new skills such as Thai boxing, cooking and dancing. You also visit an elephant sanctuary where sick, old, and very young elephants are looked after, and you go to the rice paddies to learn how rice grows in the flooded fields. On your last night there is a celebration dinner called *Khantoke*, where local people serve you traditional food.

DAYS 6–7

First thing in the morning, you fly to the famous island of *Phuket*. After lunch, you can snorkel and dive in some of the bluest waters in the world. One of the dives we organise involves swimming with sharks, but don't worry, they're not the kind that attack! On the second day you hike through magnificent countryside, go on a boat trip, and see the most beautiful sunsets in your life.

DAYS 8–9

Back on the mainland, you'll spend two nights in a floating hotel on the River Kwai and will eat in floating restaurants. You'll also visit one of the most successful conservation centres for tigers in the world.

DAY 10

Your final destination is Bangkok. Here, you'll visit the Royal Palace and see the temple of the Emerald Buddha. You can also go to the world-famous 'endless markets', where you can buy real and fake designer goods at bargain prices.

Here is what some of our teenagers said about their trip:

Jessica Barnes (aged 16)
'Everything was fantastic, but the best bit for me was on the island. While I was scuba-diving I saw some amazing sea creatures, including sharks.'

Freddy James (aged 18)
'Visiting the elephant and the tiger centres were highlights for me. They are doing great things for animal conservation.'

Sam Hart (aged 17)
'My favourite part of the trip was learning Thai boxing. It was awesome!'

Vocabulary VR p113

1. Match seven of these forms of transport with photos A–G.

helicopter	camel	hot-air balloon
lorry	motorbike	elephant	bus
underground train	boat	horse
hovercraft	bicycle	ferry

2. Match the words in exercise 1 with a–c.

   a air   b sea   c land

3. Discuss these questions.
   a Which ways of travelling do you use most often? When do you use them?
   b Which forms of transport from exercise 1 have you never used? Which would you like to try? Why?

Listening Part 2

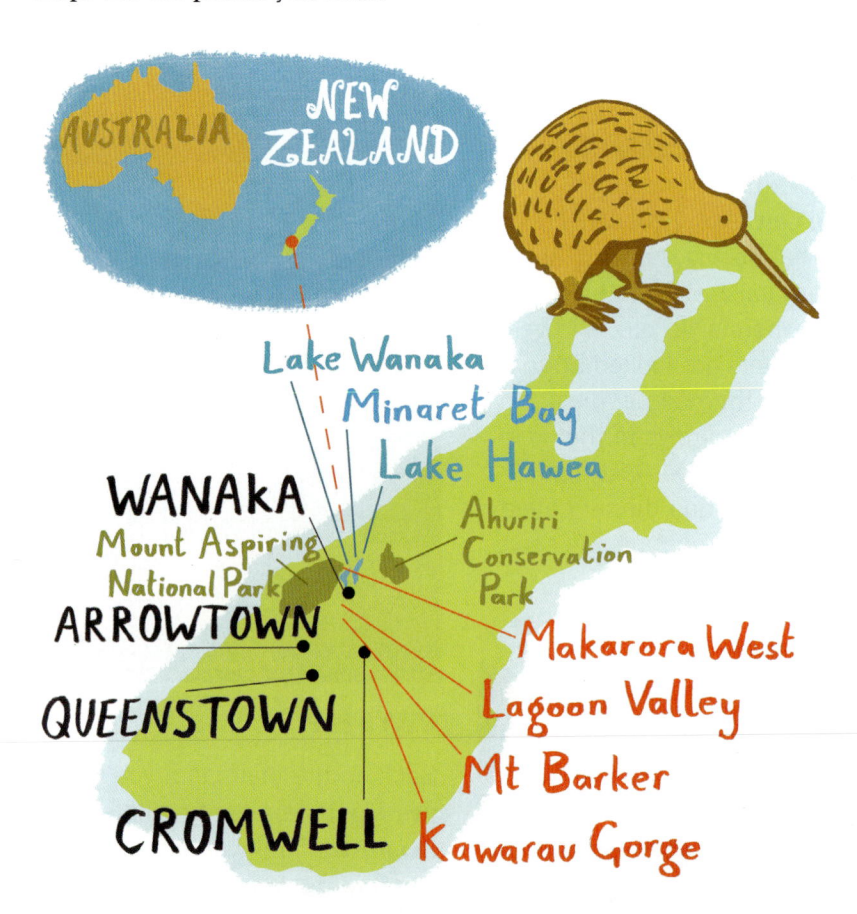

1. ▶6 You will hear a woman called Megan talking on the radio about a journey she's been on. Listen to the introduction and tick on the maps the six places you hear.

20 Unit 1

2 ▶7 Listen to the complete dialogue and for questions 1–6 choose A, B or C.

1 Megan travelled from Queenstown to Wanaka
   A on public transport.
   B in a car.
   C by plane.

2 What does Megan say about the scenery at Wanaka?
   A There are different things to see.
   B It's generally a very flat area.
   C There is very little water.

3 How did Megan travel during the trip to the glaciers?
   A by boat and on foot
   B by boat, by helicopter and on foot
   C by boat and by helicopter

4 How long does the trip to the glacier last?
   A about twenty-five minutes
   B almost four hours
   C about three and half hours

5 Megan says that the best time to take photos is when you're
   A flying above the mountains.
   B standing above the glaciers.
   C travelling across the lake.

6 How many trips to Wanaka are there every day in the summer?
   A one
   B two
   C three

3 What's the most exciting or interesting journey you've been on? Tell a partner about it.

glacier = a large mountain of ice

Grammar
The past simple and past continuous GR p121

1 Underline the four verbs in sentences a–c and name the tenses.
   a Megan went to New Zealand.
   b Megan was driving all morning.
   c I took some great photos while we were flying.

2 Complete the rules by writing *past simple* or *past continuous* in a–d.

   We use the (a).................. for completed actions in the past.
   We arrived in London yesterday.
   We use the (b).................. for past actions or situations that continued for a period of time.
   They were walking all day from morning till night.
   We use the (c).................. for actions or situations in progress in the past and the (d).................. for actions that interrupt them.
   I was waiting for my train, when I saw a friend.

3 Read the text and complete 1–15 with the past simple or past continuous form of the verbs given.

Last year, I (1).................. (go) to Australia. We (2).................. (fly) into Brisbane, but we (3).................. (not stay) there. We (4).................. (leave) the next day for an island off the east coast, and while we (5).................. (sail), a group of dolphins (6).................. (swim) very close to our boat. It was amazing! The island (7).................. (have) white sandy beaches, green forests and beautiful freshwater lakes. We (8).................. (stay) in a hotel on the beach and (9).................. (get) up early every day to watch the sunrise. The beach was beautiful and we (10).................. (enjoy) swimming and playing volleyball, but we (11).................. (not relax) like that every day. We (12).................. (do) a lot of different activities. One day when we (13).................. (explore) a shipwreck, we saw a shark. Luckily it wasn't dangerous, but I was still pretty scared. On another day, while we (14).................. (ride) horses along the beach, we saw a whale far out in the water. At night, we went on boat trips and (15).................. (feed) the wild dolphins. It was fantastic!

Listening Part 1

1 Look at the pictures in questions 1 and 2. List everything you can see in each one.

   Example   *1 A a house, fields, trees ...*

   1

   2

2 ▶8 Listen and tick the things you hear from your list.

3 ▶9 Listen to the Part 1 task. For questions 1 and 2 choose A, B or C. You will hear each question twice.

   > **tip** The speakers may talk about more than one picture but only one is the right answer.

Vocabulary VR p113

1 Look at the words in the box. Put them into groups a and b. Add two more ideas to each group.
   a things to do on holiday
   b places to stay on holiday

hotel	youth hostel	sunbathing	photography
safari	villa	cruise	sightseeing	surfing
diving	campsite	cruise ship		

2 Say where you prefer to stay on holiday and what you enjoy doing.

Speaking VR p113

Tell a partner about your last holiday. Use these ideas.
- Where did you go?
- When did you go?
- How did you travel?
- Where did you stay?
- What did you do?
- What did you enjoy most?

Vocabulary

VR p113 GR p125

1 Read this description and complete 1–7 with *a*, *an*, *the* or –.

It looks like (1).................. island in (2).................. hot country. It has (3).................. fantastic beach with (4).................. trees. (5).................. sea is clear and deep blue. I think (6).................. island is in (7).................. Greece.

2 Match these words to photos A–E. Describe three of the photos as in exercise 1.

mountain	desert	sea	wood
field	hill	river	cliff
lake	valley	coast	forest

3 Tell your partner about somewhere in your country that is popular with tourists.

Writing Part 2

1 Read Carla's postcard. Which of a–f below does she mention?

Dear Lizzie

I'm having a great time by the Red Sea in Egypt. We're staying in a really nice hotel near the beach and we've got views of the sea. Yesterday, I went diving and I saw some fantastic fish.

See you soon!

Love

Carla

a where she is on holiday
b who she's with
c where she's staying
d her plans for the next day
e what she did the day before
f a plan to meet Lizzie

2 Read the writing task below. Did Carla include everything she should in her answer?

You are on holiday. Write a postcard to an English friend. In your postcard you should

➡ say where you are on holiday
➡ describe where you are staying
➡ talk about what you did yesterday

Write 35–45 words.

3 Read the **how to do it** box, then write your own answer to the task in exercise 2.

➡ **how** to do it

Read the instructions carefully.
Make sure you know who you are writing to and why.
Include all three points.
Check the number of words you have written.

Unit 1

2 Learning

Lead in VR p113

1 Look at photos A–E below and discuss these questions.

   a What is the name of each activity or interest? Choose from:

   | wildlife   dressmaking   archaeology |
   | drawing   cookery   foreign languages |
   | drama   photography   computer games |

   b What's the best way to learn each of the activities above? Choose from:

   | the Internet   studying books |
   | going to a class   watching an expert |

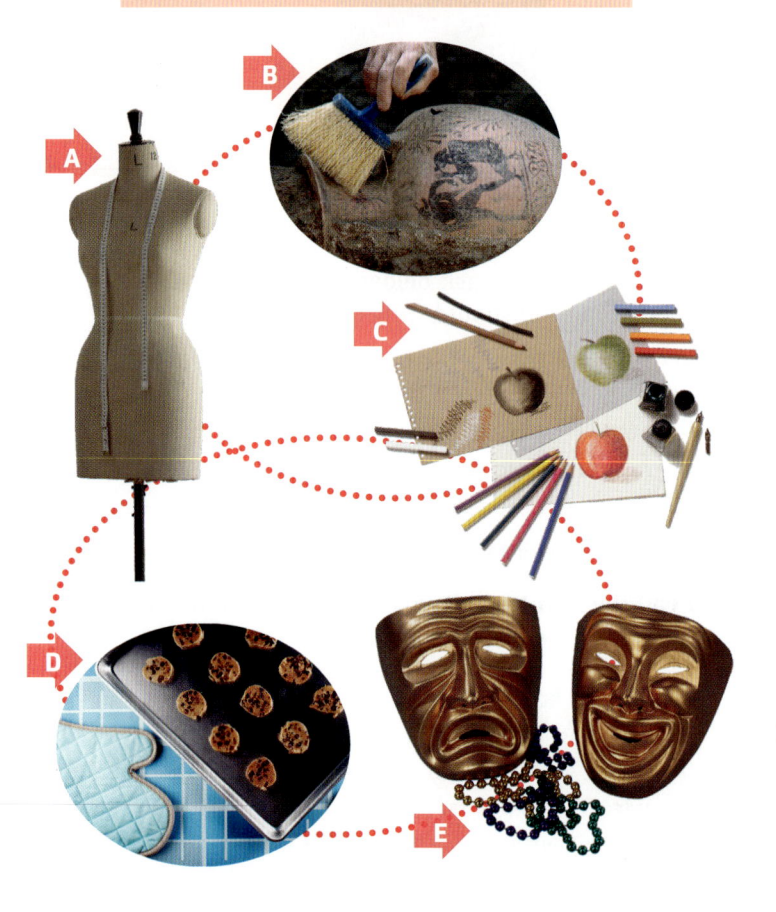

2 Tell a partner about the activities you do. Say where you do them and why you enjoy them.

Reading Part 2

1 The people in 1–5 want to learn a new skill. Read the texts and answer questions a and b for each one. Underline the answers in the texts. The first one is done as an example.

   1 Kaito wants to learn about <u>ancient history</u>. He'd like to spend <u>two or three days</u> with other people finding out about the past.
      a What is Kaito interested in? *ancient history*
      b How long does he want to spend learning about it? *two or three days*

   2 Mario and Lucia want to do something creative together. They're retired, so are looking for a class they can do regularly during the day.
      a What kind of activity do Mario and Lucia want to do?
      b When do they want to do it?

   3 Olivia is very busy and would like to learn something new at home. She's an artistic person and always prefers to work alone.
      a Where does Olivia want to learn?
      b What kind of person is she?

   4 Michael is looking for a job to do with wildlife and nature. He'd like to do a short course that will give him some useful experience.
      a What subjects does Michael want to study?
      b What kind of activity would he like to do?

   5 Ella loves socialising and often has friends over for dinner. She's looking for something she can do in the evenings after work.
      a What does Ella enjoy doing?
      b When would she like to do her activity?

2 Read texts A–H on page 25 and decide which course is most suitable for the people in 1–5 above.

   tip Look for the key information about the people expressed in different words in texts A–H.

3 Do any of the activities in A–H interest you? Why / Why not?

Unit 2

~KAITO~ ~MARIO & LUCIA~ ~OLIVIA~ ~MICHAEL~ ~ELLA~

A Learn with professionals
Would you like to draw like a professional? Well, you don't need to take expensive classes. You can learn with professionals online to draw animals and people and scenes from nature. Improve your skills when you feel like it and when you have the time.

B Join The Academy
Learning the language is a great way to understand the culture and history of a country. The Language Academy is offering a fortnight's language course in the English countryside. Choose from French, Spanish, Arabic or Chinese. Arrive on Sunday evening, meet your classmates and start learning the next day!

C Japanese Culture
Experience the best of Japan's culture while learning to cook Japanese food. We offer short courses on Saturday mornings and also during the week on Wednesdays and Fridays from 6pm–9pm. At the end of each month we make our favourite dishes and have a party.

D Be a star
Are you looking for a career in acting or do you just like acting for fun? Our drama group meets on Mondays between 12 and 2pm. We teach theatre skills and also dance. If you want to be on stage, we put on a play twice a year.

E New Look
Do you hardly ever find clothes you like in shops? Never have time to visit busy shopping centres? How about learning to make your own clothes? We hold weekend courses for dressmaking and fashion design. Courses usually last twelve weeks and include three-hour lessons each Saturday. Email now to book a place.

F Looking for Clues
Work as part of a team on a real archaeological site. We offer weekend courses for people who want to discover something about the past. Experienced professors give advice on how to use equipment to search the soil, and always provide information about what you find.

G The Taste of South America
Come to a weekend of fun and culture at the Latin Americano Hotel in the heart of the city. Come alone or with friends. Meet new people, learn to dance salsa, and try delicious South American food.

H Do something different
This amazing 'Keeper for a Day' experience allows you to work closely with some of the zoo's most popular animals. You work with a keeper to do jobs such as feeding the giraffes, cleaning the penguin pool and preparing food for the big cats.

Unit 2

Grammar
Adverbs of frequency GR p126

1 Complete the list of adverbs of frequency with these words.

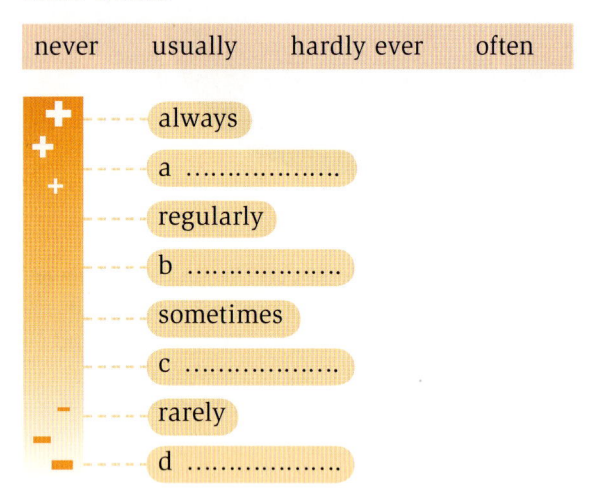

| never | usually | hardly ever | often |

- ++++ always
- +++ a ....
- regularly
- b ....
- sometimes
- c ....
- rarely
- − d ....

2 Decide where the adverbs of frequency go in a–e. More than one answer may be possible.

Example   We read magazines in our house. (hardly ever)
We hardly ever read magazines in our house.

a Our teacher is late for our lesson. (never)
b I design my own clothes. (sometimes)
c My uncle and aunt go on holiday to India. (often)
d My brother goes to his art class on Wednesdays. (usually)
e We go on holiday in winter. (rarely)

3 Make sentences that are true for you. Use the ideas in a–e and adverbs of frequency from exercise 1.

Example   play / football
I sometimes play football at weekends. I usually play with my brother but never with my parents.

a play / football
b be / late for English lessons
c have / breakfast
d go / to the cinema
e listen / to the radio

Listening Part 4

1 You will hear a conversation between a girl, Ella, and her friend, Harry, about studying abroad. Before you listen, read sentences 1–6 and say if they are about fact or opinion.

1 Ella works hard at university.
2 Harry is sorry that Ella gave up her clubs.
3 Harry will go to university next year.
4 Harry's going to do a Spanish degree.
5 Ella wants Harry to apply to her university.
6 Harry likes the idea of going to university in Spain.

2 ▶10 Listen and decide if each sentence in exercise 1 is correct or incorrect.

3 Read the audioscript on page 112 and underline the parts that answer 1–6 in exercise 1.

Vocabulary

1 Choose the correct verbs to complete a–i.

  a When you are at home and studying for an exam, how often do you *take / make / do* a break?
  b Do you think it's a good idea for students to *make / have / do* a year off before they start university? Why / Why not?
  c Have you ever *made / done / had* a language course abroad? What was it like? If you haven't, would you like to? Why / Why not?
  d Do you always *make / do* your homework on the day you get it?
  e Would you like to *do / make* a degree in languages? Why / Why not?
  f Is it a good idea to *make / do / have* some revision the night before an exam?
  g Is there any subject you'd like to *have / take / make* a class in?
  h Do you always use a dictionary when you *do / take / make* an English exercise?
  i When was the last time you *took / made* an important test or exam?

2 Work in pairs. Ask and answer some of the questions from exercise 1.

Grammar

The present simple and present continuous GR p121

1 Complete a–d with the present simple or present continuous form of the verbs.
  a I .... (write) two compositions every week.
  b My brother .... (live) in Manchester – he owns a flat there.
  c We .... (learn) about the Romans in history this term.
  d The children .... (do) their homework at the moment.

2 Match a–d in exercise 1 with uses 1–4.
  1 a regular activity
  2 a general fact
  3 something happening at the time of speaking
  4 something happening over a period of time

3 Read this advert for a language school. Correct any mistakes with verb tenses in 1–8.

(1) Are you thinking about studying English? Then come and study in one of Britain's most exciting towns!

At the Brighton School of English we (2) are teaching courses at all levels, from beginner to advanced. Most of our courses are part-time, but currently we (3) offer a new full-time course in August.

All our teachers (4) are being well-qualified, and lessons are fun and lively. Right now, we (5) recruit new teachers from Britain and the US.

Brighton's attractions (6) are including historic buildings such as The Royal Pavilion, Brighton Pier and an area of interesting and original shops known as The Lanes. Every weekend we (7) take students hiking and horse riding in the beautiful countryside nearby. In addition, this year we (8) organise weekend trips to London.

Please phone or email for more information.

Vocabulary VR p113

1 Find words below with similar meanings and put them into five groups. Check your answers in a dictionary.

> learner   coach   class
> diploma   pupil   revise
> course   learn   lecture
> professor   qualification
> undergraduate   study
> instructor   degree

2 Add at least one more word to each group in exercise 1.

Speaking Parts 3 and 4

1 In pairs, each choose one of the photos. Make notes about a–d.
   a where the people are
   b who they are
   c what they are doing
   d what else you can see

2 Take turns to describe your photo to your partner. Give as much detail as you can.

3 Discuss these questions.
   a The photographs show people learning in different situations. Which of the situations do you prefer learning in?
   b What are the advantages and disadvantages of learning in different ways?

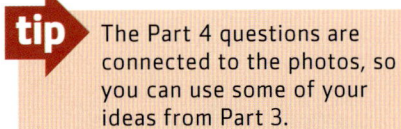

> **tip** The Part 4 questions are connected to the photos, so you can use some of your ideas from Part 3.

28 Unit 2

Writing Part 3

1 Count the number of times these punctuation marks appear in a–g below. Compare your answers with a partner.

| exclamation mark   full stop   speech marks |
| comma   capital letter   apostrophe   question mark |

a I go to the cinema every week.
b My favourite band is *Coldplay*.
c Her sister's hobby is making clothes.
d Don't touch my camera!
e Would you like to go to a concert?
f 'See you next week,' said the teacher.
g The subjects I'm best at are maths, history, and Italian.

2 Read part of a letter from Yolanda, then find and correct at least 10 punctuation mistakes in Stella's reply.

I'm learning to dance salsa! It's really good fun. In your next letter, please tell me about something new that you're learning. When do you do it? Why do you like it?

Dear Yolanda

How are you. Thank you for your letter you asked me to tell you about something new Im learning. A few months ago, I joined a drama class I go every saturday morning for three hours. The class is really informal and the teacher always gives us really interesting things to do. Every week, we do acting singing and dance. We spend one hour on each subject.

At the moment were practising a musical and well perform it at the local theatre. I can't wait for that?

I hope you and your family are well.

Love

Stella

3 Answer these questions about Stella's letter.
a What kind of class has Stella joined?
b When does she go?
c How long does the class last?
d What different skills does she learn in the class?
e What are they doing in the class at the moment?

4 Write your own answer to Yolanda's letter. Use the ideas in exercise 3 to help you. Write about 100 words.

tip Always check your work for mistakes, including spelling and punctuation.

Unit 2 29

3 Buying and selling

Lead in VR p114

1 Read sentences a–e and explain the meaning of the words in bold.

   a When do your local shops usually have **sales**? What sort of **bargains** do you look for?
   b What was the last thing you bought **at a discount**?
   c How often do you pay for things **by credit card**? What kind of things do you buy?
   d Do you keep **receipts** for everything you buy? How long do you usually keep them?
   e Does it **cost** less to shop at your local market? What sort of things can you buy there?

2 Ask and answer the questions in exercise 1.

Grammar

Countable and uncountable nouns GR p124

1 Put these nouns into the correct column below. Give the plural form of the countable nouns.

   | beef | magazine | CD player | shampoo |
   | potato | bread | grape | meat | toothpaste |

Countable		Uncountable
Singular	Plural	Singular only
stamp	*stamps*	*beef*

2 Match the items in exercise 1 with shops a–f.
   a pharmacy   d newsagent's
   b butcher's   e greengrocer's
   c baker's   f electrical store

3 Think of two more items for each shop in exercise 2. Say if they are countable or uncountable, and give any plural forms.

Reading Part 1

Read the **how to do it** box and the signs and notices 1–5. What does each one say? Choose A, B or C.

how to do it

Read each text and ask yourself: *Where is it? Who is it for? Why is it there?*
Read A, B and C carefully before you choose.
Remember, the **whole** meaning of the answer must be correct.

1

SALE
STARTS TOMORROW

HUNDREDS OF ITEMS ARE HALF-PRICE FOR SEVEN DAYS ONLY. COME EARLY!

A You can buy cheap goods here for one week.
B Everything in this store will soon be cheaper.
C It's possible to get cheap items in this shop now.

2

Restaurant closed

Please visit third-floor coffee shop for drinks and snacks

A A new restaurant will open on the third floor.
B Customers can still eat in the store.
C The coffee shop no longer serves food.

3

DO NOT LEAVE VALUABLES IN YOUR CAR. THIEVES ARE ACTIVE IN THIS AREA.

A People are advised to avoid parking here.
B The security is very good in this place.
C You should take anything expensive with you.

4

If the ticket machine is out of order please pay staff on the train

A You can only buy tickets from a member of staff.
B You must always buy a ticket on the train.
C There is a ticket machine in this place.

5

ONE CHILD EATS FREE WHEN WITH AN ADULT.
Offer applies 4–6pm on weekdays.

A Children can only eat free at weekends.
B Children can eat free before 4 o'clock on weekdays.
C Children can eat free during a period of two hours each day.

Unit 3 31

Speaking

Discuss these questions.

a How often do you shop on the Internet?
b What kind of things do you usually buy?
c What are the advantages and disadvantages of shopping on the Internet?

Listening Part 2

1 What do you think you can do on websites 1–6? Match them with a–f.
   1 *Natural Living*
   2 *Look Like a Celebrity*
   3 *Experiences*
   4 *Exchanging*
   5 *What Sounds?*
   6 *Truth about Travel*

   a find out about holidays
   b buy clothes
   c purchase 'activity' gifts for people, such as sports lessons, beauty treatments, etc.
   d find environmentally friendly gifts
   e get advice about music
   f swap things with other people

2 ▶11 Listen to someone on the radio reviewing websites, and check your answers to exercise 1.

3 ▶11 Listen again and for questions 1–6, choose A, B or C.
   1 The website *Natural Living*
      A sells items from the UK only.
      B has cheaper prices at the moment.
      C sells a lot of different products.
   2 What does the shopping website *Look Like a Celebrity* sell?
      A clothes that once belonged to the stars
      B popular designer clothes
      C similar clothes to those celebrities wear
   3 What does the reviewer say about the gifts on the website *Experiences*?
      A It can be difficult to choose a gift.
      B There aren't many ideas for gifts.
      C The best gifts are sports lessons.
   4 On the website *Exchanging* you can't
      A buy anything.
      B exchange more than one item.
      C contact people directly.
   5 The website *What Sounds?* advises people about
      A the latest music.
      B using music websites.
      C where to buy the best music equipment.
   6 From next month, *Truth about Travel* will
      A have information on more countries.
      B focus more on the best hotels.
      C allow you to book online.

4 Which of the websites do you think sounds most interesting? Why?

Grammar
Quantity GR p125

1 Read sentences a–e, which are from the Listening. Underline words or phrases showing quantity and say if the nouns are countable or uncountable.

Example *There are also <u>some</u> items from Asia and South America.* countable

a There are only a few different types of things to buy.
b How much money would you spend on them?
c There are many different ideas to choose from.
d Have you got any gifts you don't want?
e There are plenty of good travel websites around.

tip Look carefully at the words before and after the gap to help you understand what's missing.

2 Read the text about eBay and for 1–10 choose the correct answer, A, B, C or D.

	A	B	C	D
1	A lots	B many	C much	D any
2	A some	B any	C little	D much
3	A lot	B plenty	C several	D any
4	A number	B much	C plenty	D some
5	A lots	B lot	C many	D several
6	A few	B plenty	C lot	D many
7	A bit	B several	C few	D little
8	A number	B many	C much	D plenty
9	A much	B some	C many	D lot
10	A many	B much	C plenty	D lots

3 Have you bought or sold anything on eBay? Would you like to? Tell a partner.

THE SUCCESS OF eBay

There are (1)................. popular websites today and (2)................. are more successful than others. One of the best-known is eBay.

The company was started by Pierre Omidyar in 1995. As well as having a degree in Computer Science, Omidyar had had (3)................. jobs working with software and computers and (4)................. of experience in selling on the Internet. He decided to set up a page on his website to let people sell things to whoever paid the most. The idea was immediately successful and Omidyar was soon making (5)................. of money. As a result, he gave up his day job and launched eBay.

One of the things people liked about eBay was its good service. In 1999 the website stopped working for almost twenty-four hours. Although there were a (6)................. of sellers, eBay's employees called thousands of them to apologise. Omidyar also introduced a rating system. Customers were asked to spend a (7)................. time describing the service they got from others. In this way, bad sellers or bad payers were soon known.

Today eBay is used by millions of people around the world and sells almost everything you can think of. A (8)................. of items have been sold at very high prices, including a rare baseball card sold for $1.2 million. There aren't (9)................. other websites that can rival eBay and Omidyar is enormously rich. However, he and his wife have given away (10)................. millions of dollars to charity.

Vocabulary VR p114

Choose the correct verbs to complete a–e, then ask and answer the questions.

a Do you always *try on / try out* clothes before you buy them?
b What do you usually *take off / put off* first when you go to bed?
c Do you usually *get / become* dressed before or after breakfast?
d Do you always wait for your clothes to *wear out / wear off* before you buy new ones?
e What do you *put / wear* when the weather's bad?

Speaking Part 2

1 Look at photos A–E above and match them with places 1–5 in the chart.

Place	Advantage	Disadvantage
1 market	*fun and lively*	*bad weather?*
2 supermarket	*usually cheap*	*boring*
3 website	*quick and easy*	*can't see goods*
4 shopping centre	*indoors*	*many similar shops*
5 boutique	*original clothes*	*expensive*

2 Say whether you agree or disagree with the ideas in exercise 1, and why. Add more advantages and disadvantages for each place.

3 You and your friend want to buy some new clothes. Talk in pairs about the places shown and decide which is the best place to shop.

tip Try to say as much as you can about each of the photos before you make a decision.

Vocabulary VR p114

1 Look at the Fashion Wordsearch. Find
   a seven items of clothing
   b five accessories
   c four adjectives to describe style

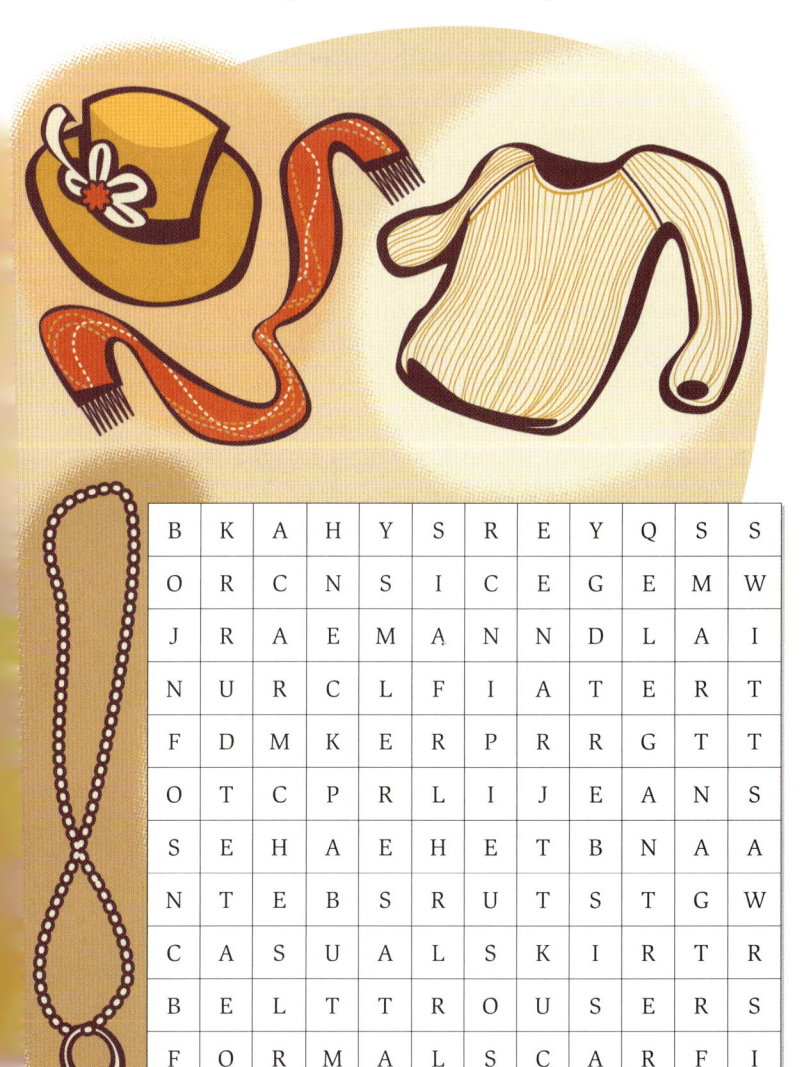

B	K	A	H	Y	S	R	E	Y	Q	S	S
O	R	C	N	S	I	C	E	G	E	M	W
J	R	A	E	M	A	N	N	D	L	A	I
N	U	R	C	L	F	I	A	T	E	R	T
F	D	M	K	E	R	P	R	R	G	T	T
O	T	C	P	R	L	I	J	E	A	N	S
S	E	H	A	E	H	E	T	B	N	A	A
N	T	E	B	S	R	U	T	S	T	G	W
C	A	S	U	A	L	S	K	I	R	T	R
B	E	L	T	T	R	O	U	S	E	R	S
F	O	R	M	A	L	S	C	A	R	F	I
O	H	A	D	N	O	M	N	E	E	T	N

Writing Part 1 and 2

1 In a–g complete the second sentence so that it means the same as the first.
   a I am really looking forward to seeing you.
      Can't ………… to see you!
   b Would you like to go to the cinema?
      Do you ………… going to the cinema?
   c We caught the number 33 bus into town.
      We ………… on the number 33 bus into town.
   d Shall we meet outside the supermarket?
      Why ………… ………… meet outside the supermarket?
   e I discovered some old photographs in my bedroom.
      I ………… across some old photographs in my bedroom.
   f I would be grateful if you would phone me tomorrow.
      Please ………… ………… a call tomorrow.
   g With very best wishes, Mark.
      Lots ………… ………… , Mark.

2 Read the task below and Ella's email. Find examples of informal language a–d in the email.
   a contractions
   b phrasal verbs
   c abbreviations
   d informal phrases and incomplete sentences

You want to go shopping this weekend in your town. Write an email to an English friend of yours. In your email you should

➡ invite your friend to come with you
➡ say what you want to buy
➡ suggest a time and a place to meet

Write 35–45 words.

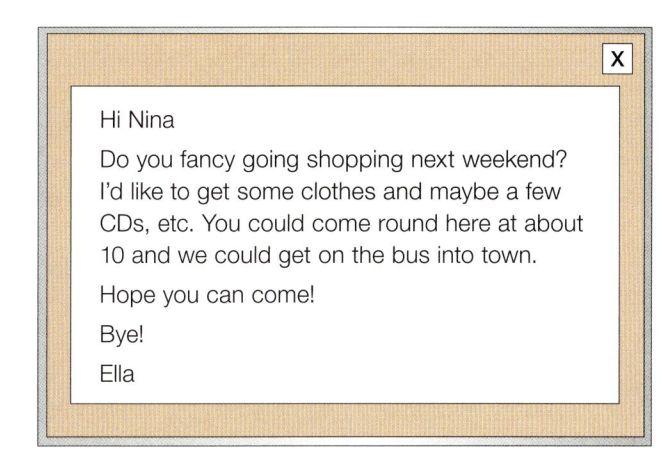

> Hi Nina
>
> Do you fancy going shopping next weekend? I'd like to get some clothes and maybe a few CDs, etc. You could come round here at about 10 and we could get on the bus into town.
>
> Hope you can come!
>
> Bye!
>
> Ella

3 Write your own answer to the task in exercise 2.

Unit 3 35

1 Review Units 1-3

1 For questions 1–8, choose the best answer.

1 Which of these travels in the air?
   A motorbike   C lorry
   B helicopter   D boat

2 Which of these always has trees?
   A a forest   C a valley
   B a desert   D a river

3 Where would you use a tent?
   A on a cruise   C in a villa
   B in a youth hostel   D at a campsite

4 Which of these interests involves food?
   A dressmaking   C cookery
   B photography   D drama

5 Which of these is a person?
   A a degree   C a coach
   B a course   D a lecture

6 Which of these do you usually do when you buy new clothes?
   A put off   C try out
   B try on   D wear out

7 Which of these do you wear on your wrist?
   A bracelet   C necklace
   B belt   D scarf

8 Which of these hasn't got wheels?
   A ferry   C bicycle
   B hovercraft   D plane

2 Choose the correct verbs to complete a–g.

a We *made / took* a vocabulary test yesterday and I got everything right.
b I'm planning to *have / do* a photography course next month.
c My sister wants to *make / take* a year off to see the world.
d We always *make / do* one or two exercises for English homework.
e How often do you *have / take* a break from studying?
f I hardly ever *take / do* any studying at weekends.
g Is your cousin *having / taking* a degree this year?

3 Find and correct one mistake in each of a–j. There may be more than one possible answer.

a I ate my breakfast when the postman arrived with a parcel.
b My brother is going to France yesterday.
c I never am late to meet my friends when we go out.
d I rarely play sport because I love it.
e Are you listening to the radio very often?
f My brother and sister watch a DVD in the living room at the moment.
g We learn to play basketball at school this term.
h I bought few CDs from the market – they're all great and a real bargain!
i There are plenty chocolates left, so help yourself.
j I don't have many money until I get paid.

4 Complete Megan's email with these words.

| diving | bicycle | ferry |
| island | sunbathing | villa |

Hi Jessica

I'm in Greece! I flew to Athens on Saturday then travelled by (1)............... across the sea to Naxos. Naxos is a fantastic (2)............... in the Aegean Sea! Yesterday we were very lazy and spent the day (3)............... by the pool. We're staying in a really lovely (4)............... . Today we went to the beach and did some (5)............... in the sea. I'd like to see more of Naxos, so I'm thinking about hiring a (6)............... and riding to some of the smaller villages. See you soon!

Love
Megan

Review 1

5 Read Sam's letter and for 1–7 choose the correct answer, A, B, C or D.

Dear Jaime

Thank you for your letter. You (1)……… me about my hobbies. Well, I have (2)……… hobbies. I like cycling, swimming and playing the guitar. I'm also really interested in archaeology and right now I (3)……… a course. At the moment we (4)……… about medieval Europe. We regularly (5)……… on trips and recently (6)……… the site of a lost village. While we were there, we (7)……… part of an old wall. It was very exciting!

Hope you are well!

Sam

1 A ask   C are asking
   B to ask   D asked

2 A lot   C much
   B several   D few

3 A am doing   C did
   B was doing   D do

4 A learn   C were learning
   B are learning   D learned

5 A are going   C was going
   B went   D go

6 A visit   C are visiting
   B visited   D visit

7 A discover   C are discovering
   B discovered   D were discovering

6 Read the task and Anna's email, ignoring the mistakes. Which sentence is not needed?

You've been on a shopping trip. Write an email to an English friend. In your email you should

➡ say where you went
➡ describe what you bought
➡ suggest meeting

Write 35–45 words.

Hi Sophie

I went shopping in Brussels last weekend, I buy some fantastic clothes in the boutiques there and plenty delicious Belgian chocolates too. I also went to some great restaurants! Do you fancy meeting in London soon! Id love to come and see you in the summer?

Bye!

Anna

7 Read Anna's email again and find
   a four mistakes with punctuation
   b two mistakes with grammar

8 Write your own answer to the task in exercise 6.

4 Animals and humans

Lead in VR p114

1 Look at pictures A–G. Which animals are shown?

2 Which of the animals shown do you think is
   a the most intelligent?   c the most like humans?
   b the most useful to humans?

3 Give examples of other animals that
   a help humans.   b are similar to humans.

Vocabulary VR p114

Match the words below with animals A–G.

| hair | tail | feather | tooth | fin |
| thumb | beak | claw | wing | hoof |

Reading Part 4

1 Read the text on page 39 to find out why it is called *The Human Spider*.

2 Read the text again carefully to find
   a the Human Spider's real name.
   b the title of his book.
   c the names of six buildings he has climbed.

3 Choose the best answer to these questions.
   1 What is the writer's main aim in writing the text?
      A to talk about Alain Robert's personal life
      B to explain why people take great risks
      C to tell readers how to do free climbing
      D to describe the climbing career of Alain Robert

   2 What would a reader learn about Alain Robert from the text?
      A He has directed a film about climbing.
      B He has never been married.
      C He has been in trouble with the police.
      D He has never hurt himself badly.

4 Discuss these questions about the text.
   a Why do **you** think he does this?
   b Would you like to do this? Why / Why not?

tip For general questions look at the meaning of the **whole** text. A word or an idea from the options may be repeated in the text, but this doesn't mean it's the right answer.

Unit 4

THE HUMAN SPIDER

A group of us stand at the bottom of Shanghai's 420-metre Jin Mao Tower. We're looking up at a figure that's climbing the outside of the building. The man climbs higher and higher until he becomes
5 a tiny dot in the distance. A woman screams, 'He's going to fall!' But he doesn't, he keeps climbing until he reaches the top. The crowd cheers. 'Who is he?' somebody asks. It's Alain Robert, also known as 'the Human Spider' and the bravest climber in the world.

10 This is not the first time Robert has climbed a building. Overall he's climbed almost a hundred, including many of the tallest skyscrapers in the world. He's climbed the Eiffel Tower, Sydney Opera House, the Petronas Towers and many, many more, but the
15 most amazing thing about Robert is that he's a free climber. This means he doesn't use any equipment. He climbs using only his hands and his feet.

In the past, Robert climbed buildings without permission and was often arrested and even sent to
20 prison. Then he became famous: film directors made documentaries about him, he wrote a best-selling autobiography called *Bare Hands* and companies paid him to climb their buildings. In 2003, Lloyds of London paid him about $18,000 to climb their
25 95-metre building. In 2004, he climbed Taipei 101 just before it opened as the tallest building in the world.

Alain Robert has fallen and broken many bones including his wrists, his nose, arms and elbow. He suffers from epilepsy* and he has a wife and three
30 children at home. So why does he continue to risk his life climbing buildings? Is it because he loves climbing? Is it because he wants to be more famous than any other climber in the world? Or is it simply because he wants to be different from
35 ordinary people?

* a disease of the brain that can cause a person to become unconscious (sometimes with violent movements that he / she cannot control)

Vocabulary VR p114

1 Find six parts of the body in the Reading text, then match them with 1–6 in the photo.

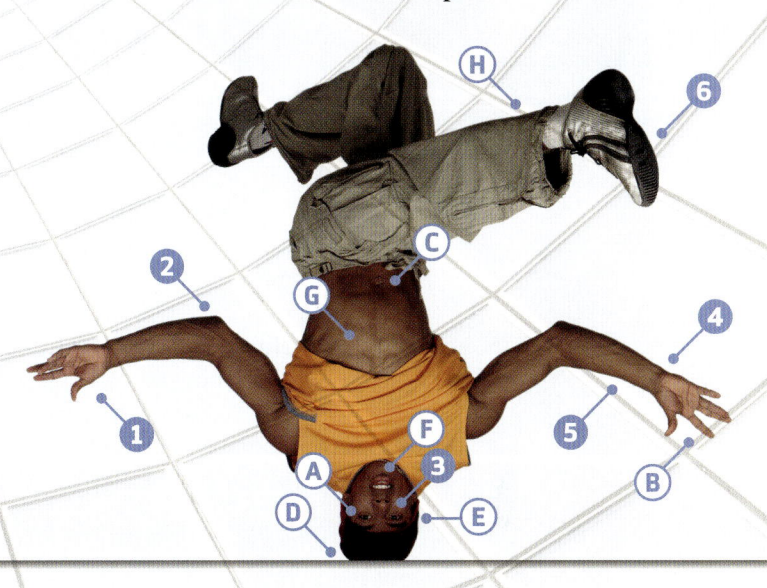

2 Match these parts of the body with letters A–H in the photo.

| stomach | mouth | eye | head |
| chest | ear | finger | leg |

Grammar

Comparative and superlative adjectives GR p126

1 Read the text below and underline three superlative adjectives and two comparative adjectives.

WOMAN LEAVES MILLION$ TO DOG

'Trouble' is one of the sweetest and most handsome dogs you can imagine. She's also one of the richest! When New York billionaire Leona Helmsley died, she left her pet $12 million. Now the little pooch is richer than most of the family. Helmsley left two of her grandchildren $5 million each while another two got nothing. In some ways Helmsley's brother was luckier than the others. He got millions of dollars, but in return, he has to look after Trouble.

2 Read the text below then complete 1–7 with the comparative or superlative form of the adjectives.

Crazy Pet Stories

It was one of the (1)............... (beautiful) weddings you could see. It took place at the (2)............... (big) nightclub in Thailand with 500 guests. The bride arrived in a chauffeur-driven Rolls Royce, wearing a pink designer gown. The groom's arrival was even (3)............... (exciting) – he came by helicopter. So, who were the happy couple? The bride and groom are a pair of rare 'diamond-eyed' cats called Phet and Ploy. Their owner spent $20,000 on their wedding making it (4)............... (expensive) than any other pet wedding ever!

But Phet and Ploy aren't the only lucky pets. In America, one of (5)............... (popular) ways people celebrate their pet's birthday is to have a party. People buy (6)............... (good) organic birthday cakes they can find and even get edible cards. And what about pet restaurants? At the Doggie Drive-Thru in Michigan, you can get cheeseburger-shaped dog biscuits. But even this isn't as funny as what happens at the Park Bench Cafe in Los Angeles. Dogs eat wearing designer clothes, sunglasses and diamond-studded collars. They're (7)............... (fashionable) than some of the best known celebrities in town!

Unit 4

Listening Part 3

1 You will hear a man talking about a pet salon in New York. Before you listen, match gaps 1–6 in the leaflet below with a–e. You will need to use one of a–e twice.

a an adjective
b a time
c a verb
d a number
e a noun

Example *3c – a verb*

New York's Top Pet Salon

All our staff have more than (1).................... years' experience

Timetable
(2).................... exercise for the dogs
9.30.   haircut and pedicure
11.00. Cats (3).................... or play
        Dogs have a bath and massage
12.30. (4).................... (please bring with you)

Cost
All cats: $50
(5).................... **dogs**: $80

Shop
Equipment for your pets
Pet food and homemade (6)....................

2 ▶12 Now listen and for 1–6 fill in the missing information in exercise 1.

Speaking Part 3

1 Work in pairs. Say what you can see in the photos. Use these words to help you.

Photo 1

| wear | dress | necklace | drink |
| cup | saucer | tablecloth | |

Photo 2

| hold | guide | help | follow |
| blind | stick | handle | |

Unit 4

Vocabulary VR p115

1 Match the film posters A–F with these types of film.

| animation | comedy | science fiction | fantasy | western |
| romance | horror | thriller | historical drama | adventure |

2 Read extracts a–j from film reviews and match them with the film types in exercise 1.
   a 'It's a very **amusing** film. I laughed from beginning to end.'
   b 'I love the bit when the **hero** and the **heroine** finally get married.'
   c 'The monsters in the graveyard were really **scary**.'
   d 'I think the **graphics** are very clever.'
   e '**My favourite scene** is the battle in space.'
   f 'It's an **exciting** story about an innocent man who escapes from prison.'
   g 'This film is **set in** Roman times.'
   h 'The wizards wore fantastic **costumes** and the **special effects** were **amazing**.'
   i 'The **main character** goes to South America in search of some hidden treasure.'
   j 'This is a **brilliant** story about a group of cowboys living on a ranch in the US.'

3 Match definitions a–j with words or phrases in bold from exercise 1.
   a clothes that actors wear to look like someone else
   b three nouns for the people in a film
   c an expression for when and where the story in a film takes place
   d unusual and exciting things done with computer tricks or clever photography
   e the part you like best
   f a plural noun that means 'computer drawings'
   g an adjective that means 'frightening'
   h an adjective that's opposite to 'boring'
   i two adjectives that mean 'really, really good'
   j an adjective that means 'funny'

Speaking

Tell your partner about a film you've seen recently.
➡ What was it called?
➡ Who was in it?
➡ What was it about?
➡ Who were the main characters?
➡ What did you like / dislike about it?

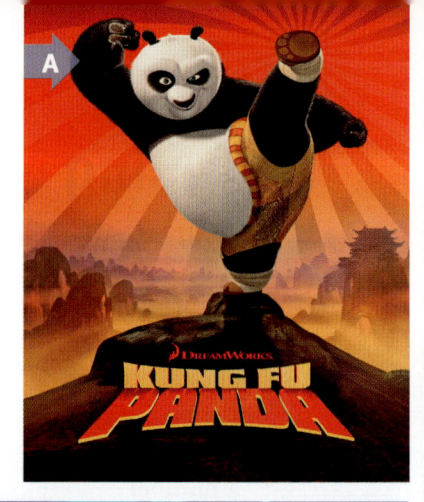

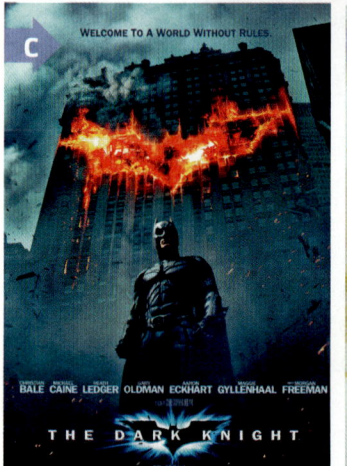

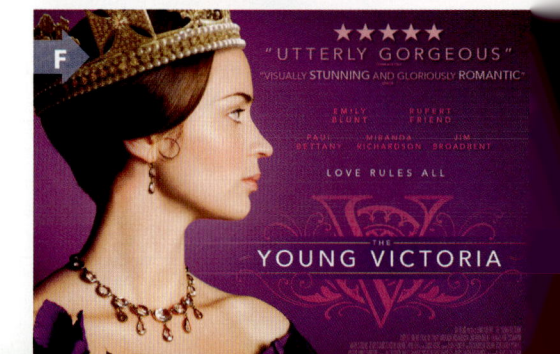

42 Unit 4

Writing Part 3

1. Read the letter opposite. Find the parts that mention a–e below. Number them 1–5 in the order they appear.
   - a   favourite scene
   - b   type of film
   - c   title of film
   - d   story and characters
   - e   reason for liking the film

2. Read the task, then answer questions a–c below.

   This is part of a letter you receive from an English penfriend.

   In your next letter, please tell me about a film you like. What's it about? Why do you like it?

   Now write a letter, answering your penfriend's questions.

   Write your letter in about 100 words.
   - a   Who are you going to write to?
   - b   What are you going to write about?
   - c   How long is your letter going to be?

3. Write your own answer to the task in exercise 2.

> **tip** Start letters with *Dear* (+ name) and a suitable beginning such as *Thank you for your letter*. Finish with a suitable ending such as *With love, Best wishes, From* (+ name).

Dear Josh

Thank you for your letter. You asked me about a film I like. 'The Wolf Man' is a horror film about an American man called Lawrence Talbot, who returns to England when his brother disappears. He discovers some terrible secrets and a strange wolf-like creature.

The original film was made in 1941. It's just as good, but I think the new film is more interesting because the special effects are better and it's one of the most exciting films I've seen. My favourite part is when Benicio del Toro first changes into the Wolf Man.

Watch this film! I sure you'd like it!

Write soon.

Miguel

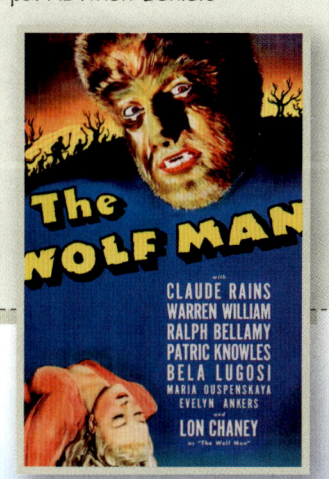

Unit 4   43

5 Health and sport

Lead in VR p115

1 Read the health and fitness advice below and complete 1–5 with these phrasal verbs.

| take up | throw away | get up |
| give up | cut down on | |

Do you feel tired all the time?
Do you often get headaches or colds?
Improve your health with this simple advice!

Eat more healthily. (1)............ unhealthy snacks such as crisps and chocolate and (2)............ fast food completely. (3)............ all the biscuits in the house and buy more fruit and vegetables.

Take more exercise. Spend less time indoors and (4)............ an exciting new sport. (5)............ earlier and go running, for example.

2 Add more advice to the text in exercise 1. Use some of the phrasal verbs and these ideas to help you.

| fizzy drinks | meat | vegetables | fish |
| sleep | water | exercise | relax | fresh air |

Reading Part 3

1 Read the article below to answer this question.
The text is about an indoor snow resort which
A is less suitable for children than for adults.
B offers different kinds of sports to try.
C has no food or shopping facilities.

Ski Dubai

Have you ever been skiing and discovered that the conditions aren't good enough to ski in? Or that you're so cold that you just want to go home? I've just come back from Ski Dubai, where there's no
05 need to worry about any of these things!

Ski Dubai's huge snowdrome, which has been open since 2005, is a building with an area of 22,500m^2 – as big as three football pitches – and it's filled with about 6,000 tons of snow all year
10 round. The snow isn't real, but is as similar to real snow as it can be. The building has an efficient cooling system, and the walls and ceilings are five metres thick so that the cold is kept inside. The temperature is maintained at around −1°C or −2°
15 C, so it never gets too uncomfortable.

As well as the comfortable temperature, you're given winter clothing and snow boots to wear, all included in the entrance price. A note on safety: all children under 12 have to wear the helmets
20 provided, but this isn't essential for adults.

2 Read the text again carefully then decide if sentences 1–8 are correct or incorrect.
1 There is always snow in the Ski Dubai snowdrome.
2 The temperature inside the building is always exactly the same.
3 You have to pay extra to use Ski Dubai's footwear.
4 Everybody has to wear a helmet in the snowdrome.
5 The snowdrome is a good area for children.
6 There is little for serious skiers to do at the snowdrome.
7 It's possible to do a skiing class at the snowdrome.
8 From the cafe you can watch people on the ski slopes.

3 Would you like to visit Ski Dubai? Why / Why not?

Inside, you can either ski or go to the largest indoor snow park in the world! It's a great place for families because you can go sledging, make snowballs and snowmen, or visit the snow cavern.

25 If you want to go skiing, there are five different levels of ski runs. This means that skiers and snowboarders of all abilities can practise their skills. The longest run is 400 metres and there's an area called the Freestyle Zone for the
30 more advanced. There's a chairlift too so you can practise your skills again and again, and there's the option of having lessons with skilled instructors.

When you need a rest, you can relax in one of the
35 cafes and watch the skiers practising. There's a shop where you can buy your own equipment, although equipment is provided in the ticket price. I've already made plans to go back next month!

Grammar

The present perfect GR p121

1 Complete a–g with the present perfect form of the verbs, then match them with uses 1–3 below.
a The match .... (finish) and the fans are pouring onto the pitch!
b Extreme sports .... (become) very popular with young people in recent years.
c .... (you / buy) a ticket for the concert tonight?
d I .... (try) surfing but I don't really like water sports.
e A new sports centre .... (open) in our town.
f We .... (see) an improvement in our football team during this year.
g My cousin .... (take part) in a lot of sports competitions.

1 experiences at a time not stated
2 recent actions that are connected with the present
3 things started during a time that hasn't finished

2 Ask and answer about a–e using the present perfect. Begin 'Have you ever ...?'
a buy something really expensive
b win a prize in a competition
c make a special meal for somebody
d ride a horse, elephant or camel
e meet a famous person

3 Write sentences in the present perfect. Put *just*, *yet* or *already* in the correct place.
a my parents / buy a new house. (just)
b your uncle / move to Switzerland? (yet)
c I / tidy my room today. (already)
d The decorators / not finish painting my bedroom. (yet)
e I /speak to our new neighbours. (just)

tip Look for different ways of saying the same thing. For example, the option may say *footwear*, but the text may say *snow boots*.

Unit 5

Speaking VR p115

Look at photos A–C and discuss these questions.
a   Do you enjoy doing sport? Why / Why not?
b   What do you think the sports in the photos involve?

Listening Part 2

1   ▶13 You will hear a woman called Sarah talking about a sport called free-diving. Read the **how to do it** box then listen and choose A, B or C for questions 1–6.
   1   What does Sarah say about the history of free-diving?
       A   It has always been an extreme sport.
       B   It was once a way of finding food.
       C   It's less than four hundred years old.
   2   What does Sarah say about free-diving today?
       A   It requires special equipment.
       B   It's non-competitive.
       C   It has several different names.
   3   How did Tanya Streeter spend a lot of her childhood?
       A   training to be a diver
       B   sailing and fishing
       C   playing in the sea
   4   Tanya realised she was a talented free-diver after
       A   she'd entered her first free-diving competition.
       B   she'd had one lesson in free-diving.
       C   she'd been doing it for a while.
   5   How does Tanya train?
       A   She exercises for five hours every day.
       B   She swims in the sea every day.
       C   She goes running every day.
   6   What advice about free-diving does Sarah give to beginners?
       A   Practise in the sea whenever possible.
       B   Take proper lessons.
       C   Enter as many competitions as you can.

   ▶ **how to do it**
   Read the instructions and questions carefully before you listen.
   Mark your answer then move on to the next question.
   Don't choose an answer just because you hear a word from the option.

2   Would you like to try free-diving or the other sports in the photos? Why / Why not?

46 Unit 5

Grammar

The present perfect with *for* and *since* GR p121

1 Write these time expressions under *for* or *since*. Add two more to each.

April	six weeks	I was a child
several years	ages	this morning
1999	five minutes	

for
....
....
....
....
....
....

since
....
....
....
....
....
....

2 Tick the correct sentences and rewrite the incorrect sentences.
   a   She's been a free-diver for the 1990s.
   b   I've been interested in water sports since a long time.
   c   We've had swimming lessons since we were very young.
   d   My family have lived on this island since ten years.
   e   They've been in the classroom since half an hour.
   f   He's been in the football team since June.

3 Read the example and a–e below, then complete the interview with a racing driver.

   Example   be interested / racing?   *ten years old*
                  Interviewer: *How long have you been interested in racing?*
                  Driver: *Since I was ten years old.*

   a   drive / racing cars?   *five years*
   b   race / this team?   *last June*
   c   know / your instructor?   *about seven years*
   d   live / Switzerland?   *teenager*
   e   own / this house?   *2007*

Unit 5   47

Speaking Part 2

1 You and your friend want to improve your health and fitness. Match photos 1–5 with notes a–e below.

a do sport
b take walks
c go on holiday
d get sleep
e eat healthy food

2 Make complete sentences from a–e in exercise 1, adding suitable adjectives and adverbs. Then say why each activity is good for you.

3 In pairs, talk about the photos. Decide which is the best way to improve your health and fitness. Use your ideas from exercise 2 and the phrases below.

> **tip** Listen to your partner's opinion and agree or disagree politely, giving reasons.

Agreeing
- I agree with you, because …
- Yes, you're right, because …
- That's true, because …

Disagreeing
- I'm afraid I don't agree, because …
- I see what you mean, but …
- That's a good point, but on the other hand …

Reaching agreement
- OK. Let's make a decision.
- Shall we come to an agreement?

Vocabulary VR p115

1 Name the sports shown in the pictures.

2 Answer questions a–g. Check your answers in a dictionary.
   a   Do you play tennis on a pitch, a track or a court?
   b   Do you play, go or do gymnastics?
   c   Do tennis players hit the ball with a racket, a bat or a stick?
   d   Does a player or a referee score goals?
   e   Does a goalkeeper or a manager save goals?
   f   In basketball, do you throw the ball into a basket, or kick the ball into a goal?
   g   Would a scuba-diver wear a mask or a helmet?

3 Complete a–h with nouns and verbs from exercise 2.
   a   Climbers should always wear a .... to protect their head.
   b   You use a .... to hit the ball in baseball.
   c   The .... always makes the final decision in a match.
   d   The .... of a team chooses which players to play in matches.
   e   Footballers play on a ....
   f   I .... swimming twice a week.
   g   How often do you .... basketball?
   h   Footballers can .... the ball or throw it from the side.

4 Say what sport this is describing.

   You play this sport on a court. There are five players in a team. You throw the ball into a basket.

5 Take turns to describe and guess different sports as in exercise 4.

Writing Part 2

1 Read the task below and Paul's email. Has he written the correct number of words?

   You have heard about a new activity at your local sports centre. Write an email to an English friend of yours. In your email you should
   ➡ describe the activity
   ➡ give details about the class
   ➡ suggest going together

   Write 35–45 words.

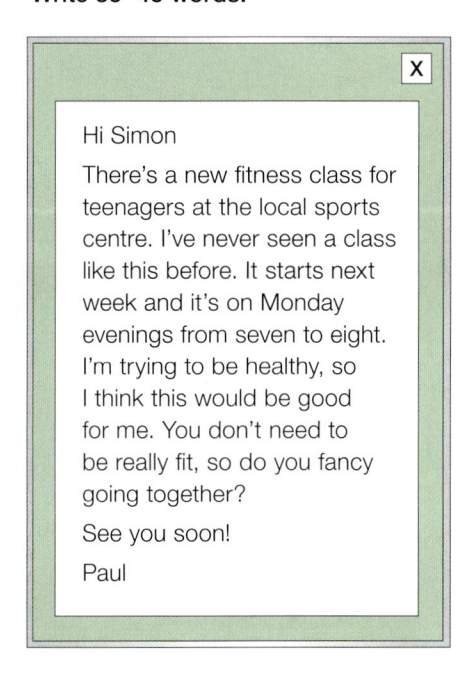

   > X
   >
   > Hi Simon
   >
   > There's a new fitness class for teenagers at the local sports centre. I've never seen a class like this before. It starts next week and it's on Monday evenings from seven to eight. I'm trying to be healthy, so I think this would be good for me. You don't need to be really fit, so do you fancy going together?
   >
   > See you soon!
   >
   > Paul

2 Underline the parts of Paul's letter which address the three points.

3 Cross out the information Paul didn't need to include. Count the number of words again.

4 Write your own answer to the task in exercise 1.

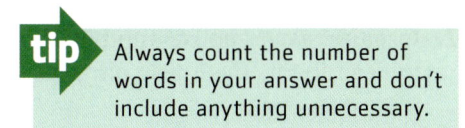

tip Always count the number of words in your answer and don't include anything unnecessary.

Unit 5   49

6 Homes and lifestyles

Lead in VR p115

1 Match this description with one of photos A–E.

   This one reminds me of a house in the jungle or somewhere children play. I think it might be uncomfortable to live in though.

2 In pairs, each choose another photo and take turns to describe it. Use these phrases to help you.
   - It looks like …
   - This one reminds me of …
   - That picture makes me think of …

3 Which of the buildings do you like most? Why?

Vocabulary VR p115

Match these words with a–d. Add two more to each group.

kitchen	town	stairs	hall
bedroom	village	countryside	
bathroom	flat	bungalow	patio
living room	balcony	city	

a location
b type of home
c room
d other features of a home

50 Unit 6

Listening Part 3

1 ▶14 You will hear a woman talking to a group of tourists at a castle. Read the **how to do it** box, then listen and fill in the missing information.

Alnwick Castle Tour

History of the castle
First built in 1096. Home of the (1)................. family since 1309.

Special features
- the (2)................. style of the drawing room
- beautiful furniture
- hand-painted china in the (3).................
- interesting paintings
- collection of (4)................. books in the library

The castle on film
- TV series
- (5)................. documentaries
- *Harry Potter* films

Worth a visit!
- cafe open for lunch
- (6)................. selling souvenirs

➡ how to do it
Read the title and the text before you listen.
Don't write too many words in each gap.
Write numbers as words or figures.
Use correct spelling if an answer is spelt out.

2 Have you been anywhere that has been on TV or in a film? Tell a partner about it.

Grammar
The past perfect GR p121

1 Read this sentence from the Listening and answer questions a–c below.

Before the Percy family moved to Alnwick, the castle had belonged to a family called De Vesci.

a Who lived in the castle first?
b Which tense do we use for the earlier event?
c Which tense do we use for the later event?

2 Correct any mistakes with verb tenses in a–e.
a I never heard of the castle until I came to England.
b During the tour, the guide told us that they built the original parts in the 11th century.
c We had to go back to the cafe because my friend left her bag there.
d After we finished the tour, we'd gone to the gift shop.
e I bought some postcards of parts of the castle I saw earlier during the tour.

3 Read the text below then complete the gaps with the verbs in brackets in the past simple or past perfect.

Last week Jaime went to Alnwick. This is what he wrote about his trip.

'I (1)................. (know) a lot about the history of the castle because I (2)................. (already / read) about it on the website. Our teacher (3)................. (also / give) us some information about it before we went. I (4)................. (go) on quite a few trips with the language school before this one, but I (5)................. (enjoy) Alnwick most. The guide (6)................. (tell) us that they (7)................. (make) *Harry Potter* films at the castle a few years earlier. I (8)................. (think) that was really interesting. As I (9)................. (wander) around the grounds, I (10)................. (try) to spot parts of the castle I (11)................. (see) in the films.'

Unit 6 51

Reading Part 2

1 The people in 1–5 below are all looking for a home to buy. Read the descriptions and find the following information about where they want to live, if stated.

a location
b type of home
c number of bedrooms

1 Ferdinand lives with his family in the countryside, but travels to the town centre every day for work. He wants to buy a one-bedroom flat close to his job, where he can stay during the week.

2 Lisa works in town but wants to live in a small house in the country. She doesn't have a car, so she needs to be close to public transport.

3 Henri and Isabelle have two children. They want to move to a house in the country that has at least three bedrooms and a big garden.

4 Jamie and Antoinette are looking for a holiday home either by the sea or in the countryside. They want to find an area that's lively and fun, where they can meet plenty of people.

5 Pieter and Dagmar are looking for somewhere to retire. They want to buy a bungalow or a flat with two bedrooms, in a quiet area of town that's close to the shops.

2 Read the **how to do it** box and adverts A–H. Decide which home would be the most suitable for each person (1–5) in exercise 1.

➡ how to do it

Read the instructions and all the information once.
Underline the key words in the people descriptions.
Make sure **all** the information matches your choice.
Check that the three texts you haven't chosen don't match any of the people.

3 Which of A–H would you prefer to live in? Why?

A This is a country cottage with views of open fields in a wonderful village location. The accommodation consists of two bedrooms, a living room, kitchen/breakfast room, bathroom and a small garden. The cottage is close to local shops and there are regular train and bus services into town.

B A large, four-bedroom, two-bathroom detached home with living room, dining room, large kitchen/breakfast room, study and double garage. The house has approximately 1,000m² of land and is in a beautiful location with views of the countryside.

C This is a three-bedroom home in a quiet area, with fantastic views of the sea. It has a small easy-to-look-after garden. There are local shops, schools and services within walking distance, and it's a thirty-minute drive to the town centre.

Unit 6

D A beautiful ground-floor apartment in a pleasant and peaceful part of the town. It has two bedrooms, a living room, kitchen, bathroom and a south-facing private garden. The apartment is five minutes' walk from the town centre and local services.

E This is a classical style villa which has just been built as part of an exciting new development. It is within walking distance of the sea, restaurants and cafes. It has three bedrooms, a large lounge, two bathrooms, fitted kitchen, garage, shared swimming pool and a small well-kept garden.

F A two-bedroom bungalow with a double garage and large garden. It's set in a delightful location close to a farm, with excellent countryside views. Just a twenty-minute drive to the local train station, which has services to surrounding towns.

G A Victorian two-bedroom terraced house situated in the fashionable heart of the town centre, within a few minutes' walk of shops, cafes, restaurants, clubs and train station. It has a fitted kitchen, living room and office, and a pretty south-facing garden. Brilliant condition!

H This is a comfortable one-bedroom third-floor apartment in a new block of ten flats, and is the last one available. The development is located within walking distance of the town centre, shops and train station. Other benefits include shared gardens and parking.

Vocabulary GR p126

1 Add missing adjectives 1–4. Be careful with spelling.

Verb / Noun	Adjective
wonder	wonderful
beauty	(1)..................
comfort	comfortable
fashion	(2)..................
imagine	imaginative
expense	(3)..................
interest	interesting
bore	(4)..................

2 Match these adjectives with their opposites in exercise 1.
a terrible   c exciting
b ugly   d cheap

3 Form the opposites of these adjectives a–j by adding -un, -in or -im. Check your answers in a dictionary.
a fashionable   f necessary
b interesting   g convenient
c expensive   h pleasant
d comfortable   i correct
e perfect   j possible

Writing

Write a short advert for your ideal home. Use Reading texts A–H and the ideas below to help you. Write about 50 words.

➡ type of home   ➡ location
➡ number of rooms   ➡ other features

Unit 6 53

Speaking Parts 1, 3 and 4

1 Look at the example then add a sentence to each answer for a–f.

Example 'Do you enjoy living by the sea?' 'Yes.'
Yes. It's really beautiful here.

a	Do you go to the beach often?	Yes.
b	Is it stressful living in a city?	Sometimes.
c	Do you have to travel far to school / work?	No.
d	Do you go out much at weekends?	Yes.
e	Is it boring in the countryside?	Sometimes.
f	Do many people live in your village?	No.

2 Read the **how to do it** box then take turns to ask and answer a–f.

a Do you live far from here?
b Do you like living in this area?
c Do you go into town very often?
d Are there many tourists here?
e Is it usually a peaceful place to live in?
f Do you usually stay here during the summer months?

➡ **how** to do it

Listen carefully to the question.
Give as much information as you can.
Use appropriate tenses.

3 In pairs, each choose one of the photos and describe it to your partner. Use these words to help you.

| busy | boring | exciting | stressful |
| peaceful | quiet | relaxing | interesting |

4 Say which place shown you'd prefer to live in and why. What are the advantages and disadvantages of where you live?

Unit 6

Writing Part 3

1 Read the writing task and Maria's answer opposite. Then answer a–e below.

This is part of a letter you receive from your new English penfriend, Amy.

I live with my parents and my sister in a house in a big town. I often meet my friends and we go shopping and to the cinema. Where do you live? What's it like? What kinds of things do you do?

Now write a letter to Amy, telling her about where you live.

Write about 100 words.

a What's the location of Maria's home?
b What kind of home does she live in?
c What activities does she enjoy?
d What's the weather like there in summer?
e How does she describe the town?

Dear Amy

Thank you for your letter. It was really nice to hear from you.

You asked me about where I live. Well, I live by the sea in an apartment on the fifth floor. I can see the sea from my bedroom window and it only takes about ten minutes to walk there. In the summer, it's usually very hot here, so I often sit on the beach and go swimming with my friends.

The town is very lively with lots of shops, cafes and restaurants. There are always a lot of tourists too.

I hope you can visit me one day.

Love

Maria

---

2 Think about your own answers to questions a–e in exercise 1. Then write your answer to the task.

tip Before you start writing, plan your ideas and decide on the best order for them.

Unit 6

2 Review Units 4-6

1 Match these words with a–g below.

adventure	balcony	bat	beak
boxing	claw	comedy	court
cycling	fantasy	feather	finger
golf	hair	hall	judo	kitchen
pitch	racket	stairs	tail
thriller	thumb	wing

a five parts of a bird
b three parts of a human
c four types of film
d four sports
e two places where you play sport
f two pieces of sports equipment
g four parts of a house

2 Complete the phrasal verbs in sentences a–e.
a I'm going to give .... fast food completely. I'm never going to eat it again!
b You should never throw .... glass bottles. You should always recycle them.
c You don't need to stop eating crisps and chocolate completely. You should just cut .... them.
d Let's take .... a new activity. How do you feel about skiing?
e Why don't you get .... earlier in the morning so that you can go to the gym?

3 Complete sentences a–j with the correct form of the word given.
a I'm surprised you enjoyed that book. I found it extremely .... INTERESTING
b I didn't sleep well last night – my new bed isn't very .... COMFORT
c Out of ten questions on the test, Pat got two right and the rest of his answers were .... CORRECT
d We had a .... view of the mountains from our hotel room. WONDER
e I'm not very .... so I can't really draw or make things. IMAGINE
f Could we meet at 7pm? 6pm is rather .... as it's a bit early. CONVENIENT
g Mitch is quite a(n) .... person and rarely says anything nice about anyone. PLEASANT
h Josie is the most .... girl at school – she even designs and makes her own clothes. FASHION
i Nobody can run faster than Usain Bolt! It's .... POSSIBLE
j Don't you think football is .... ? I do, I hate it! BORE

4 For a–h complete the second sentence so that it means the same as the first. Write no more than three words.
a Max isn't as tall as Beth.
   Beth .... Max.
b I last went on holiday in 2005.
   I .... on holiday since 2005.
c It's a long time since we've been shopping.
   We .... shopping for a long time.
d Boats are slow in comparison to trains.
   Trains .... than boats.
e I'm not as good at maths as Bob.
   Bob is .... me at maths.
f Physics and chemistry are both difficult.
   Physics is as .... chemistry.
g It's hotter in Egypt than in many other countries.
   Egypt is one of .... countries.
h We are waiting to receive our exam results.
   We .... our exam results yet.

5 For 1–12 choose the best answer, A, B or C.

1 Thrillers are .... than romantic comedies.
   A the most exciting   B as exciting
   C more exciting

2 My old computer is .... than my new computer.
   A bigger   B not as big   C the biggest

3 My cat is the .... pet in the world!
   A good   B better   C best

4 In my opinion, beach holidays aren't .... as city holidays.
   A as interesting   B more interesting
   C the most interesting

5 Have you .... been to the desert?
   A ever   B never   C yet

6 I've .... ridden a motorbike, and I don't want to!
   A yet   B never   C ever

7 The students have .... taken an exam.
   A ever   B yet   C just

8 Have you seen that new film everyone's talking about .... ?
   A just   B already   C yet

9 My cousin has lived in New York .... about three years.
   A already   B since   C for

10 When I got to school, I realised I .... my books at home.
   A left   B had left   C leave

11 We'd been on safari for about an hour when we .... our first lion.
   A saw   B had seen   C see

12 We .... at the party long before we decided to go home.
   A haven't been   B hadn't been
   C aren't

6 Read the task and the letter below and find
   a two mistakes with formal / informal language
   b three mistakes with grammar

This is part of a letter you receive from your penfriend.

I enjoy sport and I've just taken up ice hockey. I play for a local team. We train twice a week and play matches on Saturdays. Do you like any sports? Which ones do you like? Why do you enjoy them?

Now write a letter replying to Ben.

Write about 100 words.

Dear Ben Clark

Thank you for your last letter. It had been great to hear from you. The ice hockey sounds brilliant!

You asked me if I enjoy sport. Well, I live near the sea and I love surfing, so I've just joined a club. It's really good fun because the people are very nice and I've already made some good friends. I haven't been surfing on my own already, but I'm having lots of lessons. I'm already a lot best than before.

I hope you can come here one day and we can go surfing together!

I look forward to hearing from you.

Carl

---

7 Write your own answer to the task in exercise 6.

7 Art and entertainment

Lead in VR p115

Read the clues and complete the crossword.

Across
5 a large group of musicians who play various musical instruments together (9)
6 a play in which most of the words are sung to music (5)
8 a series of steps and movements which you do to music (5)
10 a work of art that is a figure or an object made from stone, wood, metal, etc. (9)

Down
1 a type of music with a strong beat, played on instruments like electric guitars, drums, etc. (4)
2 a performance of music (7)
3 a series of plays, films, musical performances, etc. often held regularly in one place (8)
4 a classical style of dancing that tells a story with music but without words (6)
7 a person that produces paintings or drawings (6)
9 a show performed in a large tent by a company of people and animals (6)

Reading Part 4

1 Read the text on page 59 about artist Duncan Hamilton. Why is it called *Disappearing Art*?

2 Read the **how to do it** box then answer these questions.
  1 What is the writer's main aim in writing the text?
    A to talk about the importance of art
    B to explain how one artist works
    C to say why ice sculpture is popular
    D to describe the disadvantages of being an artist
  2 What would a reader learn about Duncan Hamilton from the text?
    A He has always been a successful artist.
    B He makes sculptures from all kinds of material.
    C He prefers to work alone.
    D He is popular with the media.
  3 What does the writer say about the ice?
    A Duncan's team make it themselves.
    B It must be completely frozen.
    C The team have to make it quickly.
    D It is completely safe to work with.
  4 The writer says that Duncan's sculptures
    A are always huge.
    B generally last for a day.
    C take about a week to make.
    D can improve when they start to melt.
  5 Which of the following could also be a title for this text?
    A How to make an ice sculpture
    B How to change your career
    C How to get on television
    D How to make art a business

3 Have you seen any other unusual types of art?

58 Unit 7

DISAPPEARING ART

Duncan Hamilton creates great works of art, but he doesn't use paint or pencils. He's a sculptor, but he doesn't use wood or stone. He always works quickly and the longest he's ever spent on a sculpture is two weeks. So what kind of material does he use to create his art? Ice!

05 Duncan has had an interesting career. He started out as a chef and then became interested in ice sculpture. Now he has his own business, making fantastic ice sculptures for all kinds of purposes, including for the cinema, advertising, tourism and for magazine photos. Duncan has made everything from a life-size igloo in London's Trafalgar Square to a 12 metre-wide castle for a wedding, 10 and ice cubes for drink adverts.

So how does he make his sculptures? Duncan and his team work very carefully to produce their ice. This is because it has to be very clean and clear. It also has to be stored at certain temperatures. If the ice is completely frozen, it can be 15 very hard to work with. Not only that, but the ice can burn, so the artists have to wear special protective clothes.

Unlike other forms of art, ice sculptures don't last forever because they melt. Some people can't imagine losing something they've created like this. Luckily, Duncan doesn't 20 mind watching his sculptures slowly change and then disappear. Many of the sculptures even look better after a few hours at room temperature. The average ice sculpture lasts for six or seven hours and may take a couple of days to completely melt, but the smaller ones don't last long at all.

Grammar
Order of adjectives

1 Put these adjectives into the correct place in the chart below. Think of at least two more words for each heading.

red   African   huge   round   unusual   wooden   old

Opinion	Size	Age	Shape	Colour	Nationality	Material

➡ **how to do it**

Read the title and the text once.
Decide if the questions are about general or specific information.
Read the text again carefully.
Before you decide, check the other options carefully.

2 Complete these sentences with the adjectives in the correct order.
   a Maria bought a .... dress. (silk green long)
   b Harry drives a(n) .... car. (blue old horrible)
   c I had a .... meal the other day. (Greek lovely big)
   d My neighbour is a very .... man. (young French pleasant)
   e I gave my mum some very .... earrings for her birthday. (silver beautiful small)
   f She's wearing a pair of .... shoes. (leather expensive white)

Unit 7

Listening Part 4

1 ▶15 You will hear a conversation between a girl, Rosa, and her friend, Tom, about a night out. Read the **how to do it** box then listen and decide if each sentence is correct or incorrect.

1 Rosa has already heard of the musical performance *Stomp*.
2 Rosa thinks she would enjoy watching *Stomp*.
3 It was Tom's idea to see *Stomp*.
4 Tom enjoyed the whole of *Stomp*.
5 Tom is excited about going to the ballet.
6 In the end, Tom offers Rosa his ticket for the ballet.

▶ **how to do it**

Read the instructions and questions for an idea of what you will hear.
Listen for different ways of talking about 1–6.
Think about one question at a time.
Check your answers on the second listening.

2 Have you ever been to a show or other performance that you didn't enjoy? Tell a partner.

Grammar

Gerunds and infinitives GR p123

1 Match sentences a–c from the Listening to uses 1–3.
 a I can't wait to go!
 b I don't really enjoy watching ballet.
 c I'm bored of going to the same thing all the time.

 1 the gerund after certain verbs and phrases
 2 the gerund after certain prepositions
 3 the infinitive after certain verbs

2 Complete sentences a–h with the infinitive or the gerund of the verbs.
 a I can't afford .... (go) to the concert. The tickets are too expensive.
 b Did you manage .... (learn) all your lines for the play?
 c My mum refuses .... (listen) to loud music.
 d You need .... (work) hard if you want to be a professional dancer.
 e I can't imagine .... (be) a famous pop star.
 f Did you arrange .... (meet) your friends at the cinema?
 g I really enjoy .... (paint) funny pictures of people.
 h Would you mind .... (help) me move this piano?

3 In pairs, talk about a–e, using the gerund or infinitive.
 Example *a I enjoy playing football with my friends.*
 a something you enjoy
 b something you're looking forward to
 c something you can't imagine
 d something you've arranged for this weekend
 e something you've managed this month

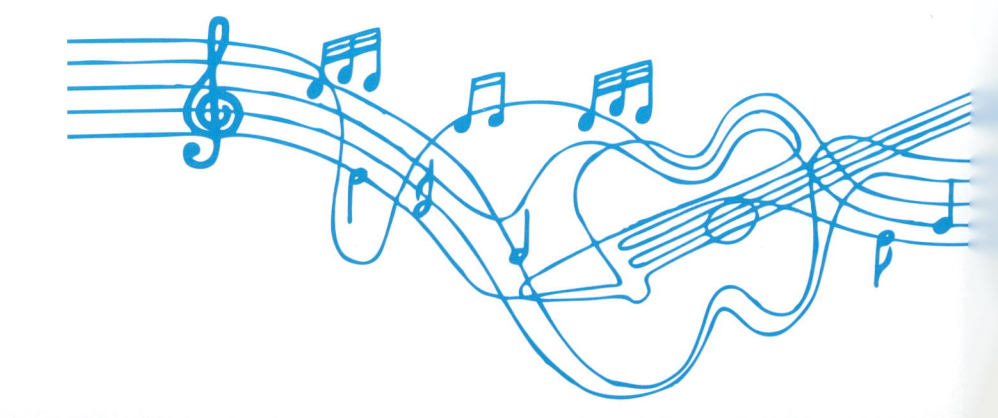

Speaking Part 3

1 Match these words with photos 1 or 2. Compare your answers in pairs.

   a costume
   b stage
   c concert
   d audience
   e village
   f sing
   g clap
   h lights

2 In pairs, each choose one of the photos. Think of at least one adjective or adverb to describe the words from exercise 1 that match your photo.

3 Read the **how to do it** box, then take turns to describe your photo to your partner.

▶ **how to do it**
Talk for as long as you can.
Describe the people, the place, etc. in detail.
Use adjectives and adverbs to make your description interesting.

Vocabulary VR p115

1 Read this review of a theatre production, then complete it with these words. There are two words you don't need.

| stage | performance | exit | audience | costumes |
| actresses | scene | entrance | play | |

Last Saturday night, local theatre company Starlight gave a powerful (1)................. of the famous (2)................. *Romeo and Juliet,* by William Shakespeare. The actors and (3)................. all showed great talent and each (4)................. was directed brilliantly. The historical atmosphere was increased by superb (5)................. and scenery. Overall it was a fantastic night out. I stood with the rest of the (6)................. and cheered at the end of the show and as I went towards the (7)................. to leave, I heard nothing but praise from the people around me. Well done Starlight!

2 Write a short review of a show or a TV programme you have seen. Include the following information:

- when and where you saw it
- who was involved
- what it was about
- what was good / bad about it

Listening Part 1

▶ 16 Read questions 1–5 then listen and choose the correct answer, A, B or C. You will hear each question twice.

1 What job does the woman do?

2 On what day does the girl want to go to the show?

A WEDNESDAY B FRIDAY C SATURDAY

3 Where will the man be tonight?

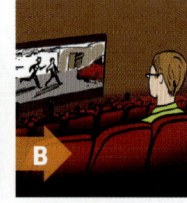

4 What instrument does the girl play?

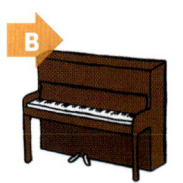

5 What present will the man buy?

Unit 7

Writing Part 2

1. Read the email from Javier and say which question it answers, A, B or C. Compare your answer with a partner.

   A Last weekend you went to a concert.
      Write an email to your friend. In your email:
      - say how much you enjoyed the concert.
      - describe the band.
      - suggest you meet up.

      Write 35–45 words.

   B Last weekend you went to a concert.
      Write an email to your friend. In your email:
      - talk about what you did before the concert.
      - say how much you enjoyed the concert.
      - describe your favourite part.

      Write 35–45 words.

   C Last weekend you went to a concert.
      Write an email to your friend. In your email:
      - say how much you enjoyed the concert.
      - describe your favourite part.
      - suggest you meet up.

      Write 35–45 words.

Hi Mike

I had a fantastic time at the Kaiser Chiefs concert last weekend. The music was great, wasn't it? I loved it when they sang Ruby and everybody joined in! The Arctic Monkeys are playing next month. Do you fancy going?

From
Javier

---

2. Match parts of the email with the three bullet points in the task you chose in exercise 1.

3. Choose one of the tasks in exercise 1 and write your own email to Mike.

8 Safety

Lead in

Look at the signs above and answer a–c.
a What do the signs have in common?
b Where might you see each one?
c What does each one tell you?

Reading Part 1

1 Read texts 1–5 and match two of them with signs from the Lead in.

2 Read the texts again carefully and decide what each one says. Choose the correct answer, A, B or C.

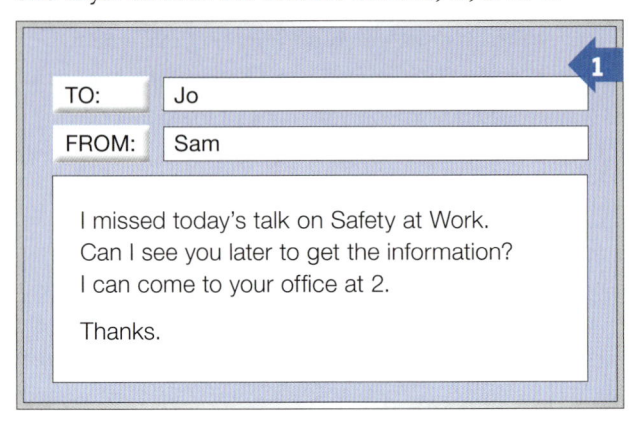

1

TO: Jo
FROM: Sam

I missed today's talk on Safety at Work. Can I see you later to get the information? I can come to your office at 2.

Thanks.

What does Sam want Jo to do?
A visit him later today
B tell him about the safety talk
C send him some information

2

ALL VISITORS MUST WEAR A SAFETY HELMET

Please report to reception to collect one.

A Any visitors can enter this area.
B Visitors should put on a safety helmet before they go to reception.
C Visitors have to get a safety helmet from reception.

64 Unit 8

Staff

Fire practices today and tomorrow at 3pm. Everyone please leave by nearest exit.

A All staff should stay in the building during the fire practice.
B There will be two fire practices tomorrow afternoon.
C All staff must leave during the fire practice.

Out of order

Please use the drinks machine in reception.

A Nobody can use this machine today.
B It's impossible to get a drink today.
C There's only one drinks machine here.

TO:	All Staff
RE:	Health and Safety

Problems with your eyesight or your back? Members of the Health and Safety Department are available today to advise you about how you use your computer.

A The Health and Safety Department must fix all computers today.
B Staff should tell their health problems to the Health and Safety Department.
C Many people in the Health and Safety Department have bad eyesight.

tip Don't choose an answer just because it includes a word or phrase from the text.

Grammar

Obligation, prohibition and necessity GR p122

1 Read sentences 1–5 and complete a–c.
 1 All visitors must wear a safety helmet.
 2 Staff mustn't stay in the building during a fire practice.
 3 All visitors have to get a hard hat from reception.
 4 Staff don't have to wear smart clothes.
 5 Children under 16 needn't buy a ticket.

 a for something it is necessary to do (obligation) we use .... and ....
 b for something you are not allowed to do (prohibition) we use ....
 c for something it isn't necessary to do (no necessity) we use .... and ....

2 Choose the correct verbs to complete a–e.
 a You *shouldn't / don't have to* tell jokes that could upset people.
 b You *have to / mustn't* wash your hands before serving customers.
 c You *mustn't / don't have to* like children, but it helps!
 d You *should / must* have a licence and enjoy travelling long distances.
 e You *don't have to / ought to* be a good speaker. You need to be heard from the stage.

3 Match the sentences in exercise 2 with these jobs.

 lorry driver   waiter   actor
 school teacher   comedian

4 Choose two of the jobs in exercise 3. Write one more sentence for each one using modal verbs of obligation or prohibition.

Unit 8

Vocabulary VR p116

1 Find 1–8 in the picture and write in the missing letters.

1 s a __ __ e __ a __
2 __ o o __ e r
3 __ e __ t l __
4 __ __ r k
5 __ __ p __ o a __ d
6 s __ __ __ n
7 p l __ t __
8 k __ i __ __

2 Find objects in the picture that are usually made of a–d.

a metal
b wood
c plastic
d glass

Unit 8

Grammar
Ability and possibility GR p122

1 Read sentences a–f and underline the modal verbs. Write A for ability and P for possibility.
   a My sister is a musician. She can play the violin and piano very well.
   b I might not study medicine at university as it takes years!
   c We may go to the park later, if we have time.
   d I think there might be a storm later; it feels very hot and humid.
   e My uncle can't work today because he's hurt his back.
   f It could rain tonight so take an umbrella!

2 Complete the rules about modals.
   a We use the verbs .... and .... (not) for ability.
   b We use the verbs .... (not), ... (not) and .... for possibility.

3 Circle six possible dangers in the picture of the kitchen on page 66. Compare your answers, then use modal verbs to say what the dangers are.

Listening Part 3

1 ▶17 Listen to a talk about safety in the home. Which two dangers in the picture on page 66 are mentioned?

2 ▶17 Read the text below, then listen again and fill in the missing information.

SAFETY IN THE HOME

Always use a fire blanket or a (1)............ cloth to put out burning oil.

Do NOT throw (2)............ onto burning oil. It might cause an explosion.

Make sure kettles, (3)............ and other electrical appliances aren't damaged.

Don't leave things like cloths and oven (4)............ close to the cooker.

Put (5)............ and frying pans on the back rings of the cooker and turn their handles away from the edge.

Make sure cleaning materials, matches and (6)............ bags are kept in cupboards.

tip Don't worry if you don't understand every word you hear. You may still be able to answer the questions.

3 Discuss other ideas for making your home safe.

Unit 8 67

Speaking Part 2

1 You're planning a walking trip in the mountains with friends. Think about what problems you might have. Brainstorm as many as possible in three minutes.

2 Look at pictures 1–6. Match each one with descriptions a–f below, then name each object.

a   very thick, strong string
b   an instrument for finding direction
c   a type of jacket that stops you getting wet
d   a small telephone that you can carry around
e   a drawing or plan of a place
f   something you look through to make distant things seem closer

> **tip** If you don't know or can't remember the word for something, say what it does or how you use it.

3 Talk to your partner about why you might need the objects shown for your walking trip, and decide which are the most important things to take.

4 Think of two other things you might need on your trip. Describe them as in exercise 2 and see if your partner can name them.

Unit 8

Vocabulary VR p116

1. Answer these questions.
   a What's the weather like today?
   b What's the weather usually like in your country in January and August?
   c What's your favourite kind of weather?

2. Match these weather words with a–c below. Add at least one more word to each group.

freezing	dry	foggy	humid	drought	cool
sunny	tornado	cloudy	wet	rainy	
blizzard	boiling	hail	snowy	flood	
hurricane	gale	lightning	thunder		

   a weather adjective
   b temperature adjective
   c extreme weather condition

3. Look at the weather forecast below and answer these questions.
   a What is the weather going to be like each day?
   b What problems might this weather cause?

   Monday
   Tuesday
   Wednesday
   Thursday
   Friday

Writing Part 3

1. Read the task and the sample answer below. Match paragraphs A–C with notes 1–3, then decide on the correct order.

   Your English teacher has asked you to write a story. Your story must have the following title:
   A dangerous situation
   Write about 100 words.

   A Suddenly Harry slipped and hurt his ankle badly. I tried to call the rescue service on my mobile phone, but there wasn't any signal. After a while, I decided to go for help.

   B When I finally arrived at the village, I contacted the rescue service and took them to Harry. He had a broken ankle, but apart from that he was fine.

   C Last weekend, I went walking in the countryside with my friend, Harry. We were staying in a village and set off early in the morning. At first, it was raining a little, but then it began to rain hard and a storm broke out.

   1 what happened in the end
   2 who was involved / when / where
   3 the main event

2. Answer these questions about the sample answer.
   a Which tenses are used? Why?
   b Which linking words are used? What do they show?

3. Read the **how to do it** box, then write your own answer to the task in exercise 1.

   ➡ **how to do it**

   Read the task carefully and think of a story that fits the title.
   Make a plan with a clear beginning, middle and end.
   Use narrative tenses and linking words to tell the story.

   Unit 8 69

9 Science and technology

Lead in VR p116

1 Name inventions 1–6 above and match each one with these categories.

  a travel and transport   c leisure
  b daily life   d science

2 Explain why each invention shown is important. Give as many reasons as possible.

3 Think of one more invention for each category a–d in exercise 1. Tell your partner why it is important and see if they can name it.

tip Remember that the statements are in the order of the text.

Reading Part 3

1 Read the text about a museum in Berlin. Which of the inventions and discoveries from Lead in exercise 1 are mentioned?

VISIT BERLIN'S TOP MUSEUMS

Berlin is well known for its nightlife, its cafes, clubs, and bars, its interesting mix of architecture and other tourist attractions. It also has many excellent museums.

THE BERLIN MUSEUM OF TECHNOLOGY

05 One of Berlin's most popular museums is the Museum of Technology. The building itself is of historical interest, as part of it used to belong to the local railway.

Apart from transport, the museum examines a mix
10 of technology through the ages. You can explore rooms full of historic printing presses, old TVs, radios, cameras, scientific instruments, telephones and much more. There's a fine collection of planes through the ages and a model of one of the world's first computers.
15 The original was built by Konrad Zuse in 1938.

The museum is divided into fourteen departments, which currently only exhibit about a quarter of the things they own. Almost every department has demonstrations and activities that make
20 learning about technology fun. Visitors can use a printing press, make paper, or watch how a suitcase is made. Children can even take a sailing lesson without leaving the museum!

LIBRARY

25 There is an excellent library at the Museum of Technology, which is open to the public, although you must apply in advance and should check opening hours.

2 Read the text again and decide if sentences 1–6 are correct or incorrect.
1 You can see a copy of Konrad Zuse's computer at the Museum of Technology.
2 Most of the items owned by the Museum of Technology are on show to visitors.
3 The Museum of Technology organises sailing courses in the nearby river.
4 You must ask before you go, if you want to visit the library.
5 Visitors can do practical experiments at The Spectrum.
6 Visitors to the museums are likely to visit them more than once.

THE SCIENCE CENTRE

30 Next to the Museum of Technology is the science centre called The Spectrum, which is definitely worth a visit. At the centre, visitors can take part in around 250 experiments in chemistry and physics, and can learn all about electricity and sound. It's a fun educational experience for
35 people of all ages.

THE SPACE MUSEUM

The Space Museum is the oldest and largest public space museum in Germany, and was set up in 1896. You can see one of the longest telescopes in the world and learn about the history of astronomy
40 and about space, the stars and the planets.

A visit to these museums will take at least a day and many people come back a second time. There is also a restaurant and gift shop.

Grammar

The passive GR p123

1 Find three passive forms in the Reading text.

2 Complete these rules about the passive using three of the items below.

| past participle | action | subject | to be |

The passive is formed with the auxiliary verb (1)................. and the (2)................. .
We use the passive when we are mainly interested in the (3)................. and not in who or what performed it.

3 Correct the mistakes with the passive forms in a–f.
a A lot of tea be grown in India.
b A painting has stolen from the art gallery last night.
c My shoes was made in Italy.
d When is X-rays discovered?
e Who was the World Wide Web invent by?
f The football cup final was saw by millions of fans.

4 Use these prompts to write questions in the present or past simple passive. In pairs, try to answer the questions.
a Who / paper / invent / by?
b Who / the Pyramids / build / by?
c Where / oranges / usually grow?
d When / mobile phones / first sell?
e Where / camels / use / for transport?

5 Match the questions in exercise 4 with these answers, then write a complete sentence for each one.
1 the Egyptians
2 in hot countries
3 in the 1970s
4 in the desert
5 the Chinese

Vocabulary VR p116

1 Match beginnings a–h with endings 1–8 to make 10 words connected with technology. Check your answers by finding the words in the Wordsearch.

B	I	M	T	S	C	R	E	E	N	E	L
N	Q	V	Q	C	X	R	D	S	O	U	Z
P	K	M	M	A	P	Q	J	O	O	S	J
X	E	K	J	L	N	D	H	M	I	O	V
P	Y	W	D	C	P	E	Y	B	N	F	H
E	B	G	M	U	D	A	X	U	S	T	I
L	O	P	O	L	Q	B	T	T	E	W	J
A	A	S	U	A	C	H	Z	E	R	A	M
P	R	P	S	T	F	R	A	J	N	R	S
T	D	T	E	O	C	W	T	C	K	E	J
O	I	A	B	R	B	O	N	Q	L	N	U
P	I	I	M	G	P	R	I	N	T	E	R

a soft   1 board
b calcul   2 een
c comp   3 top
d key   4 ware
e lap   5 uter
f mo   6 ter
g prin   7 ator
h scr   8 use

2 In pairs, take turns to choose a word from exercise 1. Explain to your partner what it does or how you use it. See if they can guess the word.

Grammar
Agreeing and disagreeing

1 Look at the examples below. Say whether A's comments are positive or negative.

A I need a new mobile phone.
B I don't.

A I don't buy expensive clothes.
B Neither / Nor do I.

A The boys don't like playing computer games.
B I do.

A Josh thinks this laptop is great.
B So do I.

2 Complete rules 1–4 with B's replies from exercise 1.

We use (1).................. to agree with a positive statement.
We use (2).................. to agree with a negative statement.
We use (3).................. to disagree with a positive statement.
We use (4).................. to disagree with a negative statement.

3 Match statements a–f with replies 1–6.
   a We think museums are interesting.
   b I'm not interested in computers.
   c Sara doesn't like science.
   d I haven't bought any computer games recently.
   e I'm going home in a minute.
   f Those students enjoy playing sport.

   1 Neither am I.
   2 I do. I really like chemistry and biology.
   3 So do we. We love it!
   4 So am I. I'll come with you.
   5 Neither have I.
   6 I don't. I think they're boring.

4 Give your own replies to statements a–f in exercise 3.

5 Discuss statements a–d in pairs. Use the example to help you.

   Example A Do you agree with the first statement?
            B Yes, I do.
            A Really? I don't. I think mobile phones are fantastic.
            B So do I, but ...

   a People spend too much money on mobile phones.
   b Playing computer games is bad for young people.
   c It's better to talk to someone on the phone than to text them.
   d The Internet is the best invention of the 20th century.

Listening Part 4

1 Discuss these questions in pairs.
   a Do you prefer emailing friends or sending text messages? Why?
   b How often do you surf the Internet? What do you use it for? Do you ever download music?
   c What new piece of technology would you most like to buy? Why?
   d Which form of technology do you think has changed modern life the most?

2 ▶18 Listen to the conversation between a girl, Rebecca, and her friend Joe. Which of the words in Vocabulary exercise 1 on page 72 are mentioned?

3 ▶18 Listen again and decide if each sentence 1–6 is correct or incorrect.
   1 Rebecca has bought two laptops in less than a year.
   2 Joe prefers Rebecca's old laptop.
   3 Joe thinks that people should buy fewer computers.
   4 Rebecca enjoys playing computer games.
   5 Joe agrees that technology has improved some things about modern life.
   6 Rebecca owns more than one phone.

Speaking Parts 3 and 4

1. These photos show students studying in different ways. In pairs, each choose a photo and describe it to your partner.

2. Two students are talking about which method of studying they prefer. Read statements a–f and match them with the correct photo.

   a 'I prefer this method because it's easier to correct things when you make a mistake.'
   b 'I like using the spell check because it means I don't need any extra books.'
   c 'I think this way is better because I don't like staring at a screen all day.'
   d 'I like using a pen and paper because it just feels better!'
   e 'It takes less time to write essays this way.'
   f 'I can write notes anytime, anywhere, in a book.'

3. Read the **how to do it** box then talk to your partner about how you prefer to study.

   ➡ **how** to do it
   Give long answers.
   Encourage your partner to speak.
   Listen to your partner and respond.

Vocabulary VR p116

1 Add *-or, -er-, -ian* or *–ist* to these words to make jobs. Check your answers in a dictionary.

photograph	art	design	bank
politics	dance	instruct	library
science	produce	music	
sail	direct	write	

2 Take turns to describe and guess the jobs in exercise 1.

Example A *This person teaches you how to do something.*
B *An instructor?*

Writing Part 3

1 Read the writing task then say which two of a–e below should include in your reply.

This is part of a letter you receive from an English friend.
I've just bought a new computer game. It's fantastic. What do you think of computer games? What kind of things do you do on your computer?

Now write a letter, answering your friend's questions.

Write about 100 words.

a describe your computer
b agree that computer games are fantastic
c say why you do or don't like playing computer games
d talk about something you've bought recently
e explain what you use your computer for

2 Read Stefan's reply to the letter in exercise 1 and answer these questions.

a Has Stefan written the correct number of words?
b Which two unnecessary pieces of information has he included?

Dear Bill

Thanks for your letter. It was great to hear from you. You asked me about computer games. Well, I don't really like playing computer games, so I don't play them very often. I bought some games last year, but I never play them.

I prefer using my computer for doing other things. My computer's quite old and I'd rather have a laptop, but never mind. I like surfing the Internet and finding interesting websites about music and things like that. I'm creating my own website at the moment which is really interesting. I also like downloading music because it's cheaper than buying CDs and I send a lot of emails to my friends.

Hope to see you soon!

From

Stefan

---

3 Write your own answer to the task in exercise 1.

Unit 9

10 Relationships

Lead in VR p116

1 In pairs, take turns to describe one of the people in the photos for your partner to guess.

2 Fill in the missing words in Joe's family tree.

William ♥ Mary
grandfather ─── (1)..........

Susan ♥ Harry   Mark ♥ Lucy
mother ─── (2)..........   *uncle* ─── (3)..........

Joe   Luke   Jane   David
ME   *brother*   (4)..........   (5)..........

3 Complete the relationships in a–f.
   a Mary is William's ...wife....... .
   b Mark is Mary's ...son....... .
   c Harry is Susan's ...Husban....... .
   d Jane is Harry's ...Daughter....... .
   e Luke is Mark's ...newfew....... .
   f Jane is Lucy's ...nice....... .

Vocabulary VR p117

1 Match these positive personality adjectives with definitions a–e below.

| kind | clever | hard-working |
| polite | brave | |

   a having good manners and showing respect for others
   b caring about others; friendly and generous
   c able to learn, understand or do something quickly and easily
   d working with effort and energy
   e ready to do things that are dangerous or difficult without showing fear

2 Match these negative adjectives with their opposites in exercise 1.
   a lazy
   b cruel
   c stupid
   d rude
   e cowardly

3 Complete personality adjectives 1–8. Say what they mean and if they are positive or negative. Check your answers in a dictionary.
   1 r __ l __ __ ble
   2 p __ t __ ent
   3 b __ s __ y
   4 f __ nn __
   5 g __ ne __ o __ s
   6 ge __ t __ e
   7 s __ cia __ le
   8 s __ l __ ish

4 Choose four adjectives from exercises 1–3. Tell a partner what makes a good friend. Give examples and reasons.

Unit 10

Speaking Part 2

1 Look at the pictures below. In pairs, discuss what kind of person would like each one as a gift.

2 You are going to buy a present for one of your teachers, who is getting married. Read the **how to do it** box, then talk about the presents in exercise 1 and decide which is the best idea.

▶ how to do it

Talk to your partner and encourage them to speak.
Discuss each picture in turn.
Talk about all the pictures in detail.
Try to reach an agreement.

Unit 10 77

Vocabulary

1. Complete a–d with the phrasal verb with the meaning in brackets. Check your answers in a dictionary.

   a. Who do you **get** .... best, in your family? (have a good relationship)
   b. How often do you **get** .... your whole family? (meet socially)
   c. Do you ever try to **get** .... family celebrations? Why? (avoid)
   d. How long do you think it takes to **get** .... a break-up with a girlfriend or boyfriend? (recover from)

2. Ask and answer the questions in exercise 1.

Reading Part 2

1. Read the five descriptions (1–5) of the people who are planning a night out. Say which of these relationships are mentioned in the texts.

   a. housemates
   b. husband and wife
   c. work colleagues
   d. same family members
   e. boyfriend and girlfriend

1 It's Ben and Kim's tenth wedding anniversary. They want to go out for a meal, but they'd also like to see a show.

2 Jessica and her sister, Helen, haven't seen each other for months. They want to go somewhere nice and quiet where they can talk about what they've been doing.

3 Matt's boss has asked him to arrange a night out for all the staff. They want music and food and aren't worried about the cost.

4 Paula and Sally share a flat and enjoy listening to all types of music. They've decided to go out for the evening, but haven't booked anything. They're planning to eat at home first.

5 Lucas and Linda have just started going out together. They'd like to go to a fun place that doesn't cost too much, where they can have something light to eat.

Unit 10

2 Read reviews A–H of places for an evening out. Decide which one would be the most suitable for the people in exercise 1.

A Enjoy your favourite Hollywood films from the 1940s and 50s every day this week at the Film Club. Pay on the night, or buy a season ticket for the week in advance, and get into every film at 50% discount. It's a bargain!

B All your favourite comedians, and some you've never heard of, perform live at the Comedy Show five nights a week. It's a fun and exciting night out. For groups of more than ten you must book in advance.

C The Red Dragon is a new Chinese restaurant with a relaxed atmosphere and friendly service. Their menu has a good choice of food at very reasonable prices. Booking is recommended for weekends.

D Enjoy the relaxed atmosphere of classical music by candlelight at the Town Hall this weekend. Listen to world-famous pieces played by one of the best-known orchestras in the world. Pay in advance or on the door.

E Sunlight ice rink is a great place to get together for an entertaining night out. Hire skates or take yours! Pay less before 9 o'clock. Hot and cold snacks available throughout the evening.

F Barracuda's is a new restaurant in town that has a modern, exciting but rather expensive menu. There is a live jazz band on Friday and Saturday nights starting at around 9.30.

G A new exhibition of modern art opens at the Arts Centre this weekend. Go along on Friday evening between 7pm and 9pm and listen to a local artist talking about her work.

H Choose from a night out at either the theatre or the opera followed by a meal in a top restaurant. This offer is not cheap but is definitely worth it for that special occasion!

3 Which of places A–H would you prefer to go to with each of these people? Why?
- friends
- your girlfriend / boyfriend
- your parents

Grammar

Possessive forms GR p125

1 Read these sentences from the Reading texts and underline four possessive forms.
 a Enjoy your favourite Hollywood films from the 1940s and 50s.
 b Their menu has a good choice of food at very reasonable prices.
 c Hire skates or take yours!
 d Listen to a local artist talking about her work.

2 Complete these dialogues using possessive forms.

Mario   Is this (1).................. concert ticket, Jaime?

Jaime   No, it isn't (2).................. . Ask John. He likes going to see live bands. It's probably (3).................. .

Teacher   Are these (4).................. football boots, boys?

Student   No, sir. They're not (5).................. . We haven't played football today.

Lizzie   Have you seen Anna? I think this is (6).................. bag.

Tom   I don't think it's (7).................. . Her bag's black, not red.

Unit 10 79

Listening Part 1

1 ▶19 Listen to the people and say what different relationships they talk about.

2 ▶20 Read the **how to do it** box. Listen to the Part 1 task and for 1–5 choose the correct picture, A, B or C. You will hear each question twice.

1 Who will the boy go out with this evening?

2 Who does the girl get on with best in her family?

3 How did the man get to the party?

4 What is the woman going to do tomorrow?

5 What is the boy allowed to buy?

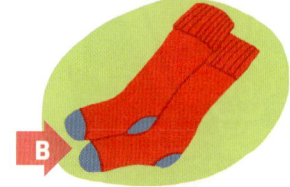

➡ how to do it

Think about each question separately.
Decide what the different pictures show.
Listen to the whole text before you choose an answer.
Check your answers on the second listening.

80 Unit 10

Grammar

The future GR p121

1 Read Chris's note then match verbs 1–7 with uses a–f below. You will need to use one of a–f twice.

> Hi Mum
>
> (1) **I'm going to visit** my friend Joe after school because I want to borrow his laptop. (2) **I'll probably be** there for a couple of hours. In the evening, (3) **I'm meeting** Lizzie at Jack's party. (4) **It starts** at 7 o'clock. Lots of people are invited, so I'm sure (5) **it's going to be** really good fun.
>
> Anyway, I've just realised I'm late so (6) **I'll give** you a ring later!
>
> Chris
>
> PS Sorry I didn't walk the dog. (7) **I'll take** him out tomorrow morning.

a general prediction
b plan / intention
c timetable / schedule
d offer
e prediction based on evidence
f decision made at the time of speaking / writing

2 Complete 1–8 with suitable forms of the verbs in brackets.

Yvonne What are your plans for the summer?
Gary (1).................. (I / visit) my cousin in Paris. Then (2).................. (we / travel) to Italy.
Yvonne Fantastic! Can I come?
Gary Why not? (3).................. (I / ask) my cousin.
Yvonne Thanks! When (4).................. (you / ask) him?
Gary Well, I can't tonight because I (5).................. (I / meet) some friends and (6).................. (we / go) to a concert. But (7).................. (I / phone) him tomorrow if you like, in the afternoon.
Yvonne Do you think (8).................. (he / say) 'yes'?
Gary Well, he's a nice guy and he's very sociable!

3 Talk about the future with your partner using the ideas in exercise 1.

Writing Part 3

1 Read the task and the model answer below. Choose the correct first sentence (a, b or c) for the story.

Your English teacher has asked you to write a story. Your story must begin with this sentence.

a I remember the day I met my girlfriend.
b I met my best friend on holiday last year.
c I had a big argument with my brother in Greece.

Write your story in about 100 words.

> .... I was on holiday with my parents in Greece. We were staying in a nice place, but there were no other young people. On our last day, I was sitting in a cafe when a really pretty Greek girl came in. She told me that her dad had a job in England and they were going to move there. Imagine my surprise when I discovered they were going to my town – Brighton. I gave her my address, and six weeks later we met in a cafe in Brighton. That was two years ago. We've been going out ever since!

2 Divide the model answer into three paragraphs. Compare your ideas.

3 Write two more sentences to follow these first sentences for stories.

a I remember the day I met my best friend.
b I woke up suddenly and looked at the clock.

4 Choose one of the first sentences in exercises 1 or 3. Make a plan in three paragraphs, then write your story.

3 Review Units 7-10

1 For questions 1–8 choose the best answer.

1 Which of these is a performance of music and singing?
   A an orchestra   C an opera
   B a sculpture   D a circus

2 Which of these is a very strong storm?
   A hail   C drought
   B hurricane   D flood

3 Which of these is used to type text onto a computer screen?
   A keyboard   C printer
   B calculator   D software

4 Which of these people helps to make the laws of a country?
   A politician   C director
   B scientist   D instructor

5 Which of these has a negative meaning?
   A generous   C cowardly
   B reliable   D polite

6 Which of these would you use to eat soup?
   A a fork   C a knife
   B a spoon   D a plate

7 Which of these describes hot weather?
   A foggy   C humid
   B freezing   D snowy

8 Which of these phrasal verbs means 'to avoid doing something'?
   A get on with   C get out of
   B get together with   D get over

2 Match these words with a–f below.

designer	wood	screen
sunny	kettle	metal	cloudy
spoon	china	mouse	cool
laptop	saucepan	plastic	banker
printer	boiling	cooker	sailor

a four items found in a kitchen
b four types of material
c four words to describe weather
d four words to do with computers
e three jobs

3 Read the text below and for 1–10 choose the correct answer, A, B, C or D.

CHOPSTICKS

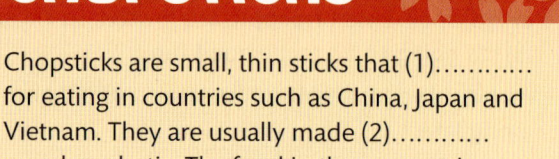

Chopsticks are small, thin sticks that (1)............ for eating in countries such as China, Japan and Vietnam. They are usually made (2)............ wood or plastic. The food in these countries (3)............ usually chopped up into small pieces, then (4)............ is brought to the table in small bowls. This makes using chopsticks easier.

Chopsticks were first used (5)............ people in China about 5,000 years ago. It (6)............ that the use of chopsticks was encouraged by the great Chinese philosopher Confucius. He was a very peaceful man who (7)............ that knives are like weapons and that chopsticks suggest gentleness.

If you visit China, you (8)............ eat with chopsticks, but it is a good idea. You should only ask for a fork if you really can't manage (9)............ chopsticks. But remember, it's much more fun if you can use (10)............ and practice makes perfect!

82 Review 3

1 A be used   C are used
   B use   D is used

2 A by   B at   C for   D of

3 A are   B be   C is   D were

4 A that B there C it   D what

5 A with B at   C of   D by

6 A is thought   C thought
   B has thought   D had thought

7 A believed   C is believed
   B was believed   D had believed

8 A mustn't   C don't have to
   B shouldn't   D can't

9 A uses   C use
   B to use   D is used

10 A their   C they
   B theirs   D them

4 Correct the mistakes in sentences a–h.
a Jessica is wearing a long beautiful red skirt.
b I'm bored of to study every day.
c You have to wear a tie, but you should be smart.
d Can you imagine to be rich and famous?
e Drivers should to drive carefully in the rain.
f Can I borrow yours pen? I've lost mine.
g I can't afford going out tonight.
h We meet in town at 2 o'clock tomorrow.

5 Complete these dialogues with the correct words. There may be more than one possible answer.
1 A I need a new computer.
   B So ………… I.

2 A I don't have a laptop.
   B ………… do I.

3 A I don't really enjoy going shopping.
   B I ………… . I love buying clothes.

4 A I love cooking fish.
   B I ………… . I hate the smell.

5 A I want to be a doctor.
   B So ………… my brother. He's studying medicine.

6 A My parents have got a new car.
   B My parents ………… . Theirs is about ten years old.

6 Read the task and the story below, ignoring the mistakes. Choose the correct first sentence for the story, A, B or C.

Your English teacher has asked to you write a story. Your story must begin with this sentence:

A I hate meeting new people.
B I had a terrible meal last week.
C I made a mistake last Saturday.

Write your story in about 100 words.

……… It was my friends birthday. We had arranged meeting at 7 o'clock in a Italian, little restaurant. When I arrived, no one was there and the waiter didn't have our booking. He said I would sit down and wait for my friends. While I was waiting, a girl came into the restaurant. I recognised her from my old school. She was with hers family, but they asked me to sit at their table. We ordered some food and I forgot about my friends'. Then as we were coming out of the restaurant, I saw theirs. They were coming out of the pizzeria opposite.

7 Read the email again and find
a two punctuation mistakes
b five grammar mistakes

8 Choose A, B or C in exercise 6 and write your own story.

Review 3 83

11 The natural world

Lead in VR p117

1 Match problems 1–4 with photos A–D.
  1 People **dump** rubbish into the seas, rivers and **oceans**.
  2 **Litter** can be dangerous for **wildlife**.
  3 Traffic causes **air pollution** and increases **global warming**.
  4 People **cut down** trees in the rainforests and destroy the **natural habitat** of animals.

2 Match words in bold in exercise 1 with a–d.
  a the natural home of a plant or an animal
  b pieces of paper, rubbish, etc. that are left in a public place
  c to get rid of something that you do not want, especially in a place which is not suitable
  d the increase in the temperature of the earth's atmosphere, caused by the increase of certain gases

3 Give definitions for the remaining words in bold from exercise 1. Check your ideas in a dictionary.

Reading Part 4

1 Read the article on page 85 about an environmental story. What do these dates and numbers refer to?
  1992   29,000   10,000   3,000

2 Read the text again and answer questions 1–4.
  1 What is the main purpose of the text?
     A to discuss the problem of rubbish in our seas
     B to talk about how some plastic ducks have helped scientists
     C to suggest how ships can avoid losing what they are carrying
     D to explain the way water moves in the ocean
  2 What does the writer say about Dr Ebbesmeyer?
     A He is interested in ocean currents.
     B He is very worried about the environment.
     C He is angry with the shipping company that lost the ducks.
     D He has travelled to most parts of the world.
  3 What does the writer say about the ducks still at sea?
     A There are very few left.
     B They are all heading in the same direction.
     C They are in very bad condition.
     D They are no longer useful.
  4 Which of these is the best headline for a newspaper article about the story?
     A Plastic Ducks Cause Wildlife Disaster
     B Plastic Bath Toys Change Pollution Laws
     C Ducks Give Important Information About Global Warming
     D Lost Toys Found At Last

PLASTIC DUCKS LOST AT SEA

In 1992, a ship travelling from China to the US was hit by a storm in the middle of the Pacific Ocean. Its cargo of containers was washed overboard and
05 at least one of them split open. The container held around 29,000 yellow plastic ducks as well as plastic frogs and turtles. The toys floated out into the water and have been travelling across the oceans ever since.

10 It isn't unusual for things from ships to get lost in the sea. Every year, as many as 10,000 containers fall into the ocean, spilling out everything from sports shoes to plastic bricks. These objects have already done harm to both our seas and our wildlife, and if the accidents don't stop, the situation will get worse. However, in the case
15 of the floating ducks, something positive has happened.

Scientists know that the direction in which water moves in our seas and oceans affects our climate. Dr Ebbesmeyer, a scientist in the US, realised that observing the ducks as they float around the world can help us understand how ocean currents work. In order to collect
20 information, he began to track the ducks' progress; predicting where they would go, and listening to reports of where they were found.

It seems that after travelling together for some time, the ducks went in different directions. Many of them floated south to the shores of Indonesia, Australia and South America. Meanwhile, the rest headed
25 north into the Arctic Ocean, becoming trapped in ice until the winds and the movement of the water sent them over 3,000 kms to the North Pole.

Today, although many ducks have been found washed up on different shores around the world, thousands of the ducks are still floating. So,
30 if you see a plastic toy, bleached and worn after so much travelling, with the words 'First Years' printed on it, and you report your find, you will help towards our understanding of the world's climate.

Grammar
Zero and first conditional GR p122

1 Make complete sentences by matching a–f with 1–6.
   a If we don't protect endangered animals,
   b If global warming continues,
   c You save water
   d There won't be enough oxygen
   e If we eat more organic food,
   f If it doesn't rain for a long time,

   1 ice in the Arctic will melt.
   2 if you take shorter showers.
   3 some of them will become extinct.
   4 there's sometimes a drought.
   5 we'll probably be healthier.
   6 unless we protect the rainforests.

2 Look at the sentences in exercise 1.
   a Which are zero conditionals and which are first conditionals?
   b Do you agree with the first conditional sentences?

3 Complete a–e using the first conditional and your own ideas.
   a If they cut down trees in the rainforests, …
   b Global warming will get worse if …
   c If we leave litter on beaches, …
   d Air pollution will increase if …
   e You'll save electricity if you …

tip Make sure the whole answer you choose is correct, not just part of it.

Unit 11   85

Vocabulary

Read the two extracts below from newspaper stories and complete gaps 1–8 with these prepositions.

| about | on | in | for | of | from |

Over the years, destruction to the Great Barrier Reef has been blamed (1)................... tourists and divers who took pieces of coral as souvenirs and damaged the coral by standing on it. Today, many conservationists are involved (2)................... trying to stop further destruction. One of their measures is that they insist (3)................... keeping tourists away from many parts of the reef in order to protect it (4)................... further damage.

A dedicated teams of conservationists who believe (5)................... changing the world and looking after our environment have had a success story. In 1997, the total number of rhinos in the wild consisted (6)................... 8,000 white rhinos and 2,500 black rhinos. Today there are more than 14,000 white rhinos and nearly 4,000 black rhinos. Now conservationists are hoping (7)................... similar successes with other endangered animals. If you want to learn (8)................... these projects, take a look at the WWF website. It's a great place to start.

Grammar

Second conditional GR p122

1 Complete a–f to make second conditional sentences.

a If I .... (have) enough money, I'd be a space tourist.
b If I went on safari, I .... (love) it!
c If I .... (be) you, I wouldn't worry!
d I .... (buy) my own yacht if they were cheap enough.
e If something large from space .... (hit) the earth, it could damage it.
f If I had the chance to travel to the moon, I .... (be) very excited.

2 Use your own ideas to complete these second conditional sentences.

a If I won the lottery, ...
b If I saw a ghost, ...
c If I failed my English exam, ...
d If I was very tall, ...

3 Read the **how to do it** box, then for 1–5 complete the second sentence so that it means the same as the first. Write no more than three words.

➡ **how to do it**

Read the first sentence and think of a way of saying the same thing.
Look carefully at the words before and after the gap.
Make sure the tense and form of any verbs are correct.
Check that your answer has exactly the same meaning as the first sentence.

1 If we want to save the environment, we need to stop using so much energy.
   We won't save the environment .... we stop using so much energy.
2 You should take care of your health.
   If I were you, ... care of my health.
3 If you don't study hard, you won't succeed.
   You won't succeed unless .... hard.
4 Ice cream doesn't freeze unless you put it in the freezer.
   If you .... ice cream in the freezer, it doesn't freeze.
5 I'm really worried about global warming, because I live by the sea.
   If I didn't live by the sea, I .... so worried about global warming.

86 Unit 11

Listening Part 2

1 What kind of litter do you think there is in space? Where do you think it comes from?

2 ▶21 Listen to an interview with journalist Adam Green. Which two of these statements are true?
   a Adams has always had an interest in space.
   b The amount of space litter is increasing.
   c Space litter never falls to earth.

3 ▶21 Listen again and for 1–6 choose A, B or C.
   1 Adam first became interested in space when
      A he was asked to write about Edward White.
      B he discovered an interesting story.
      C he spoke to an astronaut.

   2 Adam did his research by
      A interviewing people.
      B investigating on the Internet.
      C reading about the subject.

   3 What surprised Adam about the rubbish in space?
      A Some of it comes off spacecraft.
      B There is so much ordinary rubbish.
      C Astronauts drop most of it.

   4 Rubbish causes so much damage in space because
      A it's often very large.
      B it travels very quickly.
      C it's usually made of strong material.

   5 What does Adam say about the number of accidents in space?
      A There are more than he expected.
      B The amount is growing.
      C There haven't been many yet.

   6 What happened to spacestation Skylab as it fell to earth?
      A The whole thing fell into the sea.
      B It broke into two pieces.
      C Parts of it landed in different places.

Vocabulary

1 Complete the phrasal verbs in a–g with these verbs. You'll need to use one of them twice. Check your answers in a dictionary.

| pick | run | turn | give | cut | fill |

a Why is it good to ……………… **off** the tap when you brush your teeth?
b Is it bad to ……………… **on** the TV just because you're bored?
c Do you think it matters if we ……………… **down** trees in the rainforest?
d If you see litter, do you ……………… it **up**? Why / Why not?
e Do you think we'll ever ……………… **out of** resources like oil and gas?
f Should people ……………… **up** their cars with petrol less often? Why / Why not?
g Would you ever ……………… **up** eating meat? Why / Why not?

2 Ask and answer the questions in exercise 1.

Speaking Parts 3 and 4

1 Work in pairs. Each choose one of the photos below and make notes. Use these prompts to help you.
- Who?
- Where?
- When?
- What?
- Why?

2 Take it in turns to describe your photo to your partner.

3 The photos on page 88 show ways that ordinary people can help look after the environment. Read questions a–d then match two of them with answers 1 and 2 below.

   a   Is it important to look after the environment? Why / Why not?
   b   Should we give up using cars? Why / Why not?
   c   Does it matter if people drop litter? Why / Why not?
   d   How can we create less waste?

   1   In my view, leaving rubbish in public places looks horrible, and can be dangerous for wildlife. If people do it they should get a fine. Then they should be told to go and pick up rubbish in the park or from the beach.
   2   In my opinion, people should definitely use public transport more often and they should walk more. Walking is far better for your health. But I don't think you can tell them to stop driving altogether. Driving is too much a part of daily life.

4 Work in pairs. Take turns to ask and answer questions a–d in exercise 3. Use these expressions.

   Giving your opinion
   ➡ In my view / opinion …
   ➡ I (don't) think / believe …
   ➡ As far as I'm concerned …

   Asking your partner's opinion
   ➡ What do you think (about that)?
   ➡ How about you?
   ➡ What's your opinion / view?

Writing Part 3

1 Read the task and Elena's answer below, ignoring any mistakes. What environmental issue does Elena write about? What does she do to help?

This is part of a letter you receive from an English friend.

We're doing a project on the environment at school. What are the environmental problems in your country? Have you ever done anything to help? What?

Now write a letter answering your friend's questions.

Write about 100 words.

> Dear maria,
>
> Thanks for your letter. It was great to hear from you.
>
> You wantid to know about some of the environmental problems in my country. In my opininon, the worst thing is air pollution. There is too many cars in our citys. If people use their cars less, it wouldn't be so bad.
>
> Last month, I buy a bike and now I cycle to school every day. This is much better for the environment and it keeps me healthy two?
>
> Write soon!
>
> Elena

2 Find nine mistakes in Elena's answer. Look for mistakes with grammar, spelling and punctuation.

3 Write your own answer to the task in exercise 1.

tip If you're not sure what to write, use your imagination.

Unit 11   89

12 Food and celebrations

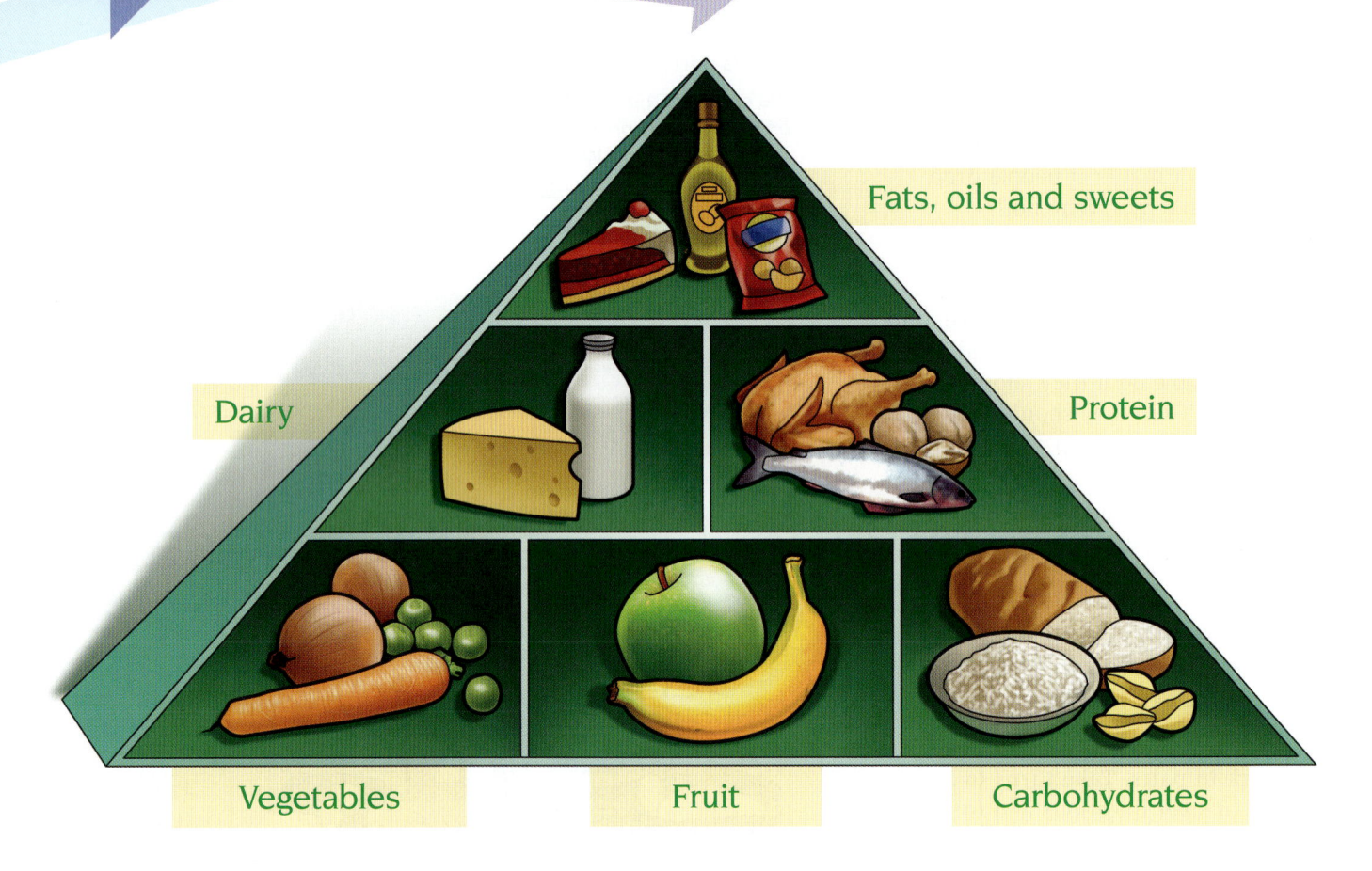

Fats, oils and sweets

Dairy

Protein

Vegetables

Fruit

Carbohydrates

Lead in VR p117

Answer questions a–d about the food pyramid above.

a Name the foods shown. Add at least three more to each section.
b Which groups of food do you like best / least on the food pyramid?
c Which groups of food do you need to eat most / least of according to the food pyramid?
d Do you think you have a balanced diet? How do you think you could improve your diet?

Vocabulary VR p117

1 Complete a–f with these words in their singular or plural form.

cup	packet	slice	bar	spoonful	glass	bowl

a How many .... of sugar do you have in your tea or coffee?
b How often do you have a .... of cereal in the morning?
c How many .... of bread do you eat every day?
d Do you ever have a .... of coffee in the afternoon?
e How many .... of water do you drink a day?
f Would you rather have a .... of crisps or a .... of chocolate?

2 Make more phrases with the words in exercise 1.

Examples a cup of tea
a slice of cake

3 Ask and answer the questions in exercise 1 and add more of your own.

90 Unit 12

Reading Part 1

1 Read texts 1–4 below and find a–c.
   a one notice on the wall of a cafe or a restaurant
   b one email
   c two labels on packets of food

2 Read the texts again. Decide what they say and choose the correct answer A, B or C.

1 EAT WITHIN THREE DAYS OF OPENING

A You can eat this food up to three days after opening the packet.
B This packet contains enough food to feed three people.
C Unopened packets of this product must be thrown away within three days.

2 After opening, keep in a cool, dry place and use within three months. DO NOT REFRIGERATE.

A This product must be stored somewhere cool immediately.
B This product can last for three months after you've opened it.
C This product needs to be kept in a refrigerator at all times.

3 FREE soft drink with every pizza ordered.

A You can have a free pizza with every order.
B You don't pay for any drinks when you order a pizza.
C You get something free when you order a pizza.

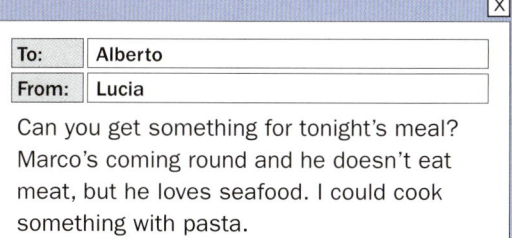

4
To: Alberto
From: Lucia

Can you get something for tonight's meal? Marco's coming round and he doesn't eat meat, but he loves seafood. I could cook something with pasta.

Lucia wants Alberto to
A cook tonight's meal.
B buy some seafood.
C eat at Marco's house.

Grammar

Comparative and superlative adverbs GR p126

1 Read a–d and underline the words and phrases used to make comparisons.
   a Is Moroccan food cooked more slowly than other foods?
   b I can cook a bit, but Luis cooks much better than me.
   c Indian food isn't cooked as quickly as Chinese food.
   d The children all eat a lot but Sarah eats the most noisily!

2 Complete a–d with these phrases, and the correct form of the words in brackets.

| as ... as   more ... than   less ... than   the most |

   a I work .... (hard) my friends. In fact, I probably work even more than them.
   b I'm happy to say that I speak English .... (fluent) I did last year.
   c Jake drives .... (fast) he used to. In fact he drives quite slowly now.
   d Tom talks .... (loud) in our class.

3 Complete the second sentence so that it means the same as the first. Write no more than three words.
   a My brother is the best cook in our family.
      My brother cooks .... anybody in our family.
   b I don't speak Italian as well as my sister.
      My sister speaks Italian .... than me.
   c Megan sings more beautifully than anybody.
      Nobody sings .... Megan.
   d Most people don't drive as carefully as my parents.
      My parents drive .... than most people.
   e I train harder than everyone in the team.
      Everyone in my team .... than me.

Unit 12 91

Listening Part 4

1 ▶22 Listen to a conversation between two friends, Joe and Claudia, about a meal at a restaurant. Note down five adjectives that describe the taste of food.

2 ▶22 Listen again and decide if each sentence 1–6 is correct or incorrect.
   1 Joe was surprised that he liked the food at the restaurant.
   2 Joe enjoys cooking food from different countries.
   3 Claudia has met Joe's flatmate.
   4 Claudia knows what a traditional Moroccan starter is.
   5 Claudia enjoys eating meat.
   6 Joe thinks Claudia should try the restaurant.

3 Discuss these questions.
   a What's your favourite place to eat? Why?
   b What are the most traditional dishes from your country? What are they made from?
   c What food from other countries do you enjoy?
   d How often do you cook? What kind of food do you make?

Grammar
Reported speech GR p123

1 Look at how these statements from the Listening have been reported. Then answer questions a and b.
   1 Joe said, 'The salads are fantastic.'
      Joe said that the salads were fantastic.
   2 Claudia said, 'I've never eaten Moroccan food.'
      Claudia said that she had never eaten Moroccan food.

   a What happens to the verbs in reported speech?
   b What happens to the pronouns in reported speech?

2 Rewrite a–c in reported speech.
   a Joe said, 'Luis is planning to work in a top French restaurant.'
   b Joe said, 'We went to that new Moroccan restaurant in town.'
   c Joe said, 'We'll probably go quite soon.'

3 Look at how statements 1–4 have been reported, then answer a–c below.

1 Claudia asked Joe, 'Did you go to an Indian restaurant?'
Claudia asked Joe if / whether he had been to an Indian restaurant.

2 Claudia asked Joe, 'What did you eat at the restaurant?'
Claudia asked Joe what he had eaten at the restaurant.

3 Claudia said to Joe, 'Take me with you next time!'
Claudia told Joe to take her with him next time.

4 Claudia told Joe 'Don't leave it too long!'
Claudia told Joe not to leave it too long.

a Which of the reported sentences are commands?
b What happens to the word order in reported questions?
c What happens to the word order in reported commands?

4 Choose the correct verb to complete each sentence.

a Harry *said / told* that he liked Spanish food best.
b My teacher *asked / said* me where my homework was.
c Sam's parents *told / said* him to tidy his room.
d My friend *told / asked* me if I wanted to go for a meal.
e I *said / told* my sister not to touch my belongings.
f Jen *said / asked* she would phone me soon.
g I *asked / told* my mum if she would make me a sandwich.
h George *told / said* he wasn't hungry.

Speaking VR p117

Ask and answer these questions.

a Do you prefer sweet things like chocolate and biscuits, or salty food like crisps?
b Do you like hot and spicy food like curry?
c Do you prefer milk chocolate or dark, bitter chocolate?
d Do you like the taste of lemons, or are they too sour for you?
e Do you enjoy things with a fishy taste like seafood, or do you prefer meat?

Vocabulary

1 Name the celebrations shown in photos 1–4. Choose from these:

| a wedding   a birthday   Christmas Day |
| New Year's Eve   Easter Day   Mother's Day |
| Thanksgiving   Valentine's Day   Hallowe'en |

2 Match the celebrations in exercise 1 with these descriptions.
   a It's the last day of December.
   b In some countries, people eat chocolate eggs on this day.
   c Children dress up as ghosts and monsters on this day.
   d It's the day when people give one of their parents special cards and flowers.
   e It's a day when people in love celebrate.
   f This day is an American celebration of food, and it takes place in November.
   g This is when a couple gets married.
   h It's when you celebrate the day you were born.

3 Complete the text with these words.

| bride   church   honeymoon   presents |
| reception   speeches   bouquet |
| bridesmaids   groom   wedding   confetti |

In Britain, many people get married in a (1)................... or in a registry office. Guests are invited and they bring (2)................... and cards. The (3)................... often wears a traditional long, white dress and carries a (4)................... of flowers. She usually has two or three (5)..................., who wear special dresses too. The (6)................... wears a smart suit and has a best man, who looks after the (7)................... ring. After the wedding, the guests throw (8)................... over the couple as they leave. Then they all go to a big party called a (9)..................., where they eat, cut the wedding cake and listen to (10)................... . The married couple often go away on a holiday, called a (11)................... .

4 What usually happens at weddings in your country?

Speaking Part 2

Tell your partner about another popular celebration in your country. Say
- why it's celebrated
- where it's celebrated
- who takes part
- what people wear / eat / do

Writing Part 3

1 Read the task and the answer below. The ending is missing. Who do you think knocked at the door?

Your English teacher has asked you to write a story.
Your story must have the following title:

A happy celebration

Write your story in about 100 words.

> It was my eighteenth birthday. I had a party at home and invited all my friends. We put up decorations and made some fantastic food. I was a bit sad because my boyfriend, Jim, was away. He was travelling in Africa.
>
> Then there was a knock at the door.
> 'It's Jim,' I cried. 'He's come home!'
> I ran and opened the door.

2 Read these possible endings to the story. Decide which is the best one, and say why.

A It was my best friend. 'Sorry, Amy,' she said. 'I got a letter from Jim. He said he never wants to see you again.' I told my guests to go home.

B It was a group of my friends. They had some presents for me. 'Thanks,' I said. 'Come and have some food.' The party ended at ten o'clock.

C It was the postman. He had a parcel from Jim. Inside, there was a beautiful gold necklace, a pair of gold earrings and a huge card. I was very happy after that!

3 Write your own story for the task in exercise 1.

> **tip** Make sure your story fits with the title you've been given. If you are asked to write a happy story, don't give it an unhappy ending.

Unit 12

13 TV and media

Lead in VR p117

Find 12 words in the Media Wordsearch. In pairs, explain the meaning of each one. Check your answers in a dictionary.

P	D	O	R	C	H	A	N	N	E	L	Y
H	C	J	C	Y	P	I	S	O	M	P	W
O	N	O	A	E	R	N	T	G	A	R	E
T	E	U	M	C	E	T	U	A	G	O	A
O	W	R	E	M	S	L	E	E	A	G	T
G	S	N	R	R	E	B	S	A	Z	R	H
R	P	A	A	A	N	N	C	E	I	A	E
A	A	L	M	D	T	E	T	R	N	M	R
P	P	I	A	I	E	S	T	A	E	M	M
H	E	S	N	O	R	H	V	D	T	E	A
E	R	T	J	D	I	Q	C	R	T	O	N
R	P	A	P	A	R	A	Z	Z	I	E	R

96 Unit 13

Listening Part 1

1 ▶23 Listen to the people and say which words connected with the media you hear.

2 ▶24 Listen to the Part 1 task. For questions 1–5 choose A, B or C. You will hear each question twice.

1 Where did the girl leave her magazine?

2 How did the man find out about the traffic news?

3 How will the boy see the film?

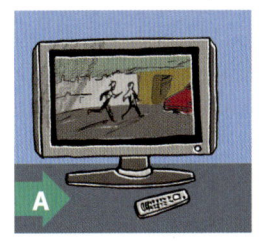

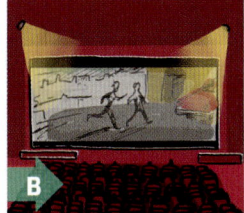

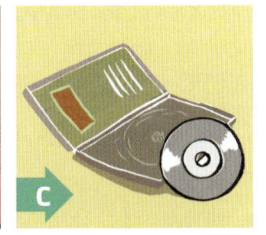

4 When will the man's son be in the newspaper?

5 What time is the man's sister on TV?

Speaking Part 1

1 Read the examples. Then add two more sentences to each reply in 1–4.

Examples

Q Do you enjoy watching TV?
A Yes, I do. I really like watching films and documentaries. I also like comedy shows and quizzes.

Q Do you ever listen to the radio?
A No, I don't. I usually listen to music on my computer or MP3 player, and I get the news from the Internet. I don't really like any radio programmes.

1 Q Would you like to be famous?
  A Yes, I would.
2 Q Do you often buy newspapers?
  A No, I don't.
3 Q Do you read the news on the Internet?
  A Yes, I do.
4 Q Have you ever met a famous person?
  A Yes, I have.

tip Make sure you use the right tense to answer the questions.

2 Ask and answer a–f in pairs. Give as much detail as possible in your replies.

a Why are you learning English?
b Have you ever been to an English-speaking country? Where?
c Do you ever watch films or TV programmes in English?
d Which actors from your country do you like?
e Do you prefer listening to the radio or watching TV? Why?
f Which are the most popular TV stations in your country?

Reading Part 4

1 You are going to read an article about a television researcher. Before you read it discuss these questions.

   a What sort of work do you think this involves?
   b What sort of person would enjoy this job?
   c What skills might be useful?

2 Read the text, then for each question choose the correct answer, A, B, C or D.

Working in TV

Have you ever thought about working in TV? How about being a researcher? Researchers have interesting jobs that generally involve finding
05 the information, the people and the places to make television, radio and film shows. They may have to research information for a documentary, for example, or find a studio audience and
10 guests for quiz and chat shows.

There are different ways to become a researcher, but this is how Louise Hamilton began. 'I studied French and Spanish at university and then
15 worked for a year at the BBC's News Bureau in Madrid. I saw an advert for a programme in London that needed Spanish speakers to help with research, so I applied for the job.' Many
20 researchers do courses in Media, but Louise didn't feel she needed to. 'The research and communication skills I learned at university were all I really needed.'

25 Louise says that there's not a typical day at work. It depends what type of programme you're working on. With documentaries, for example, you start in the office talking to people on the
30 phone. Later, you go out and help the rest of your team with the filming. 'You must be able to work as part of a team,' says Louise. 'We all have different jobs and we all need each other.'

35 What's the worst thing about being a researcher? 'It's the long hours,' says Louise. 'I used to work too hard. I didn't use to have a social life. These days I'm a little more relaxed.' And the best
40 thing? 'You can meet really interesting people, such as when you're working behind the scenes at a concert or interviewing politicians.'

And her advice to people who want
45 this kind of career? 'Do any job, however boring, and work on any type of programme. You also need to understand that, although working on TV isn't always glamorous, it's a really
50 interesting and often exciting job.'

> **tip** It may help to answer questions about the whole text last.

1 Why has the writer written this text?
   A to talk about TV careers in general
   B to describe a particular job in TV
   C to advise against working in TV
   D to explain what sort of people work in TV

2 What would a reader learn about being a TV researcher?
   A Most of the research is done in an office.
   B The work is quite repetitive.
   C The work involves talking to a lot of different people.
   D It's necessary to work alone for long periods of time.

3 What does Louise say about her early career?
   A She learned some of her research skills at university.
   B She left university before she'd finished her degree.
   C She learned Spanish in Madrid.
   D She trained as a researcher in Madrid.

4 According to the text, what's the best way for somebody to become a researcher?
   A Only do work that you find interesting.
   B Take any job you are given.
   C Think carefully about the kind of programmes you want to work on.
   D Learn at least one foreign language.

5 According to the writer, which of these best describes the job of a TV researcher?
   A an exciting and varied job that's never boring
   B a stressful job with long hours alone and little communication with others
   C a job that gives you opportunities to travel around the world and meet people
   D a job for those who enjoy working hard and meeting new people

Grammar
used to GR p121

1 Read the sentences about Louise and answer a and b.
   I used to work too hard.
   I didn't use to have a social life.

   a Does she work too hard now?
   b Does she have a social life now?

2 Look at the pictures and a–h below and write sentences about Joe, as in the Example. Use *used to* and *didn't use to*.

   Examples *He didn't use to work in an office, but he works in an office now.*
   He used to have long hair, but he hasn't got long hair now.

   a work in an office   e have long hair
   b wear a suit   f have an earring
   c work with actors   g use a camera
   d have children   h be married

3 Take turns to ask and answer about what you used to do or be like when you were younger. Use these ideas to help you.
   ➡ free time
   ➡ friends
   ➡ holidays and travel
   ➡ food

   Example *Did you use to watch a lot of TV?*
   Yes I did. I used to watch TV every day after school.

Unit 13

Speaking

1 An interviewer on a chat show has prepared some questions for a musician. Complete 1–7 with the correct question words or phrases.

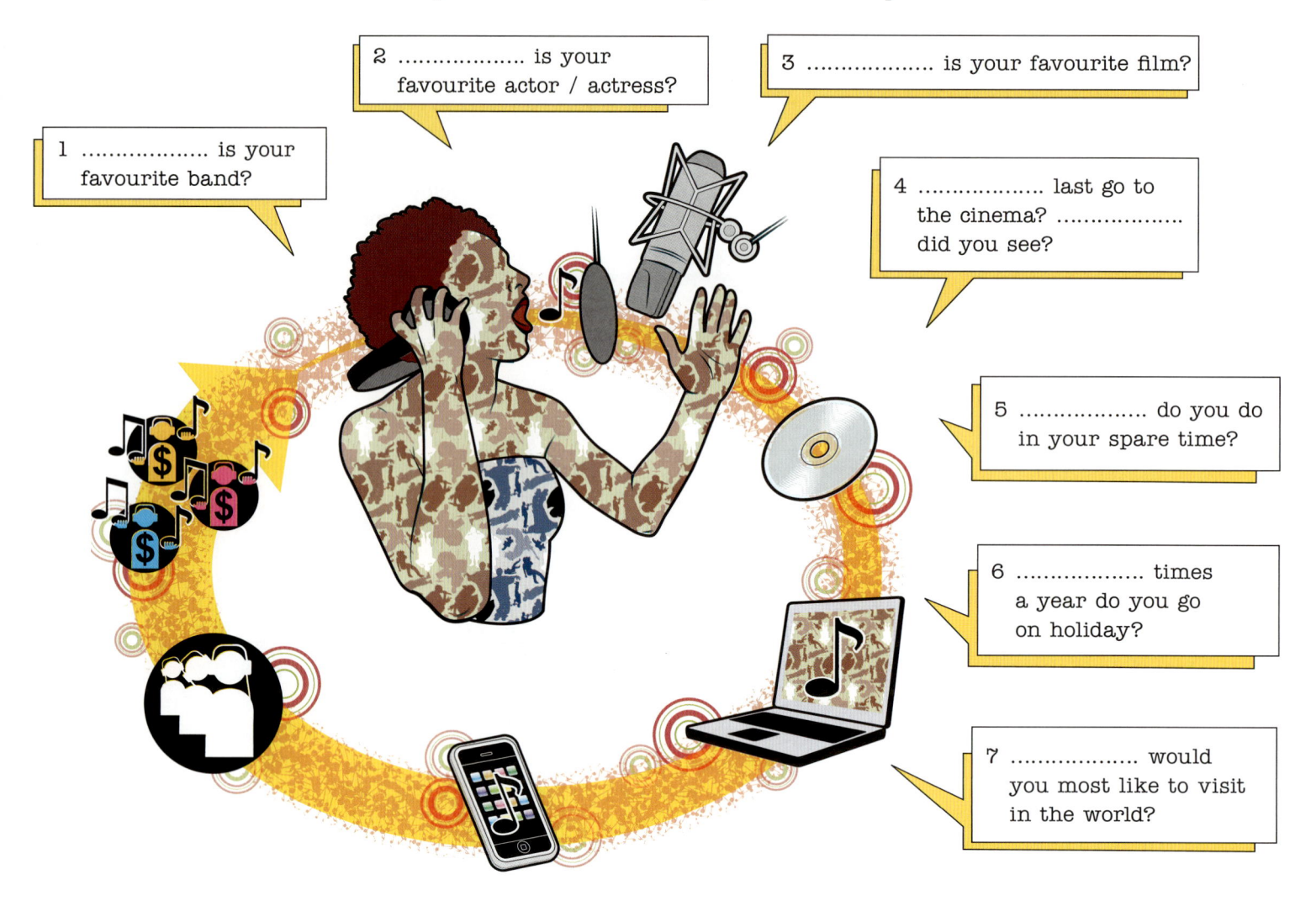

1 .... is your favourite band?

2 .... is your favourite actor / actress?

3 .... is your favourite film?

4 .... last go to the cinema? .... did you see?

5 .... do you do in your spare time?

6 .... times a year do you go on holiday?

7 .... would you most like to visit in the world?

2 Match some of the questions in exercise 1 with these answers.

a I love doing all kinds of things, but my favourite activity is probably skiing. I try to go skiing once or twice a year.

b That's difficult. I like lots of different people, but my favourite is probably Johnny Depp because I really like his films.

c I'm very lucky because it's usually two or three times a year. Last year, I went to Africa for six months. It was a great experience.

3 Role-play the interview in exercise 1 in pairs. Answer the questions and add more of your own.

Unit 13

Vocabulary VR p117

1 Match these programmes with their main features a–g.

> chat show   quiz show   reality TV show
> soap opera   documentary
> the weather forecast   wildlife programme

a information about animals, birds, insects, etc.
b facts or information about a particular subject
c real people in real situations
d a story about the lives of a group of people shown several times a week
e well-known people talking about themselves
f games, competitions and questions
g how much wind, rain, sun, etc. is expected in the next few days

2 Take turns to describe and guess different types of programmes by saying what their main features are.

Writing Part 2

1 Read the writing task and Pablo's answer below. Match the underlined words in the task with what Pablo writes.

You saw a really good programme on TV last night. Write an email to an English friend of yours. In your email, you should

➡ say what type of programme it is
➡ describe what it was about
➡ suggest something else for your friend to watch

Write 35–45 words.

Hi Pam

Thanks for your letter. It was great to hear from you.

I watched a fantastic documentary on TV last night. The programme showed how people use the Internet for communication. Did you see it? Anyway, there's another programme on tonight that I think you'd like. It's on at 8 o'clock and it's about how newspapers work.

Speak soon!

Pablo

---

2 Match a–f with synonyms 1–6.

a went to   1 discovered
b very interesting   2 chatted
c found   3 huge
d talked   4 lovely
e very big   5 visited
f very nice   6 fascinating

3 Think of synonyms for a–f. Compare your answers.

a really liked
b very small
c very funny
d well known
e noticed
f didn't like

4 Write your own answer to the task in exercise 1.

tip Try to use a range of vocabulary in your answer, don't just repeat the words from the task.

Unit 13   101

14 Communicating

Lead in VR p117

1 Look at photos 1–6 and say what different ways of communicating they show.

2 Read situations a–f below. Discuss the best way to communicate in each case and give reasons.

Example *You want to break up with your boyfriend / girlfriend.*
'You should tell them face to face. You certainly shouldn't send a text or an email because it's not personal enough.'

a You're going out for a meal tonight. You don't need your parents / flatmate to cook for you.
b You want to apply for a job advertised in the newspaper.
c You need to tell your teacher that you haven't done your homework.
d You want to invite all your friends to your birthday party.
e You need to make a dentist's appointment.
f You're organising an end-of-year party at college and want everyone to know.

3 What other ways of communicating can you think of?

Reading Part 1

1 Look at texts 1–4 and say what type of message each one is.

1
> To   Jack   X
> From   Belinda
>
> I'm sorry, but I can't make the film this afternoon. I'm having the house painted, and the decorators are still here. Do you fancy lunch tomorrow instead?

What does Belinda want to do?
A eat in a restaurant this afternoon
B change her arrangement with Jack
C avoid going out with Jack

2
> Kate – there are some sandwiches in the fridge if you're hungry. I'll be back later this evening.   Mum

What is Kate's mum suggesting?
A Kate should make sandwiches for both of them.
B Kate needs to buy something to eat this evening.
C Kate can have the food that her mum has prepared.

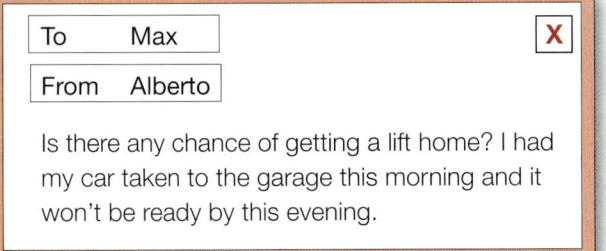

3
> To   Max   X
> From   Alberto
>
> Is there any chance of getting a lift home? I had my car taken to the garage this morning and it won't be ready by this evening.

Alberto wants Max to give him a lift because
A he doesn't like driving.
B he hasn't got a car at the moment.
C he's working somewhere different this week.

4
> To: Bart   From: Yukimi
>
> Bart – Jess will be late because she's having her eyes tested at the optician's this afternoon. She'll be here at around six.

A Jess will meet Bart at the optician's.
B Jess has had to cancel her arrangement with Bart.
C Jess is going to be delayed today.

2 Read the messages again. What does each one say? Choose the correct answer, A, B or C.

Grammar

have something done GR p123

1 Find three examples of the causative (*have something done*) in the Reading texts and answer these questions for each one.
   a Who is having something done?
   b Who is doing the action?

2 For 1–5 complete the second sentence so that it means the same as the first. Write no more than three words.
   1 Someone cut my hair last week.
      I had ………………………………. last week.
   2 Someone's designing his new house at the moment.
      He ………………………………. his new house designed at the moment.
   3 Someone's going to fix my computer tomorrow.
      I ………………………………. my computer fixed tomorrow.
   4 Someone cleaned their house yesterday.
      They ………………………………. cleaned yesterday.
   5 Someone will repair my bike next week.
      I ………………………………. my bike repaired next week.

Unit 14

Speaking

1 Discuss these questions.
- Have you or someone you know ever had an interview?
- What was it for?
- What did you / they wear?
- What happened?

2 What advice would you give to someone going for a job interview? Think about these ideas.
- speaking
- body language
- clothes
- facial expression
- time of arrival

Listening Part 3

1 ▶25 Listen to a man called Robert Kyle giving advice to a group of students about having an interview. Which of your ideas from Speaking exercise 2 does he mention?

2 ▶25 Listen again and fill in the missing information.

SUCCESSFUL INTERVIEWS:
A talk by Robert Kyle

TOPIC
How to communicate during interviews for college, university, jobs and (1).................

TIPS ON SPEAKING
Speak slowly and (2).................. and look at all the people who are interviewing you.

A smile will make you seem (3).................. and relaxed.

STATISTICS
People usually make a decision about someone after only (4).................. of meeting.

Their impressions are made up like this:

body language / clothes (5).................. %;
the way you speak and what you (6).................. is less important.

tip If the answer is a figure, you can write it in words or numbers.

Unit 14

Grammar
Expressing purpose

1 Underline the words that are used to show purpose in these sentences.
   a I'm here today to talk about having an interview.
   b Arrive early so that you give a good impression.
   c Practise what you are going to say in order to feel more confident on the day.

2 Read the **how to do it** box. Then read the text below and for 1–10 choose A, B, C or D.

WHAT SHOULD I WEAR TO MY JOB INTERVIEW?

Wearing the right thing to an interview is important **(1)**.................. order to create the right impression. Think about what you're going to wear at least a week before your interview so **(2)**.................. you can relax. If you're going for a job interview, you can stand outside the office or shop **(3)**.................. what the people who work there are wearing. If you're going for an interview at a college or a university, you can talk to your friends **(4)**.................. find out what they're wearing to their interviews.

If you can't afford something new, don't worry. Wear what you have, or borrow something from a friend. But make sure you **(5)**.................. it cleaned in time. It should be ready to wear in order **(6)**.................. to cause problems on the day. Generally, it's best to wear smart, formal clothes for a job interview. However, it's also important to wear comfortable clothes **(7)**.................. that you feel relaxed. If you're going for a less formal job, or an exam interview, it may be OK to wear jeans, but make sure they're smart in **(8)**.................. not to seem too casual. The day before your interview, go to the hairdresser's and have your hair **(9)**.................. . Some people like to **(10)**.................. their nails done too. These little things make you look and feel better.

	A	B	C	D
1	on	at	in	so
2	this	these	that	those
3	see	to see	seeing	saw
4	of	for	at	to
5	make	do	have	go
6	no	not	nothing	none
7	since	so	because	as
8	line	turn	time	order
9	cut	to cut	cutting	cuts
10	paint	do	get	cut

> **how to do it**
>
> Read the title and the text before you look at the options.
>
> Look at the words before and after the gap.
>
> Think of a word which fits the gap before you look at the options.
>
> Check that your answer fits the meaning and grammar of the sentence.

Unit 14   105

Speaking Parts 3 and 4

1 In pairs, each choose one of the photos and describe it to your partner. Say how the people might be feeling and why.

2 The photos show different people talking in public situations. Read questions 1–3 and choose the best answer for each one.

1 How do you feel about talking in class?
   a I don't like it very much because I get a bit embarrassed when I make mistakes. But if everybody is friendly and the teacher is nice, it isn't really a problem.
   b I like talking to my friends at lunchtime and after school. They all say I'm a really talkative person.

2 Do you mind talking to new people? Why / Why not?
   a I don't mind talking to people. I like going to parties. I enjoy talking to new people all the time.
   b I'm a sociable person, so I don't have any problems going out and making friends. I quite like talking about myself and also finding out about others.

3 Would you enjoy a job which involved explaining things to young people? Why / Why not?
   a That would be OK, because I quite like the idea of teaching. I suppose I enjoy helping people learn things that I already know. I don't think I'd be nervous about that kind of thing.
   b Maybe. I don't really know because I've never tried it.

3 Say what is wrong with the answers you didn't choose in exercise 2. Think about these ideas.
   ➡ Does it answer the question?
   ➡ Does it include enough detail?
   ➡ Is it long enough?
   ➡ Does it include a range of structures and vocabulary?

4 Choose two of the questions from exercise 2 and discuss them with your partner.

Vocabulary VR p117

1 Say how the people in the pictures might be feeling and why. Use these adjectives to help you.

angry	bored	cheerful	confident
delighted	frightened	tired	happy
miserable	glad	embarrassed	nervous
excited	positive	lonely	relaxed

2 Choose adjectives from exercise 1 to say how the people in a–f are feeling.
   a 'I think I'll pass my driving test.'
   b 'I'm going on holiday tomorrow.'
   c 'My boyfriend arrived three hours late!'
   d 'I've been invited to a great party!'
   e 'This film is too long and nothing happens.'
   f 'I got 100% in my English exam.'

3 Ask and answer these questions. Give real or invented answers.
   a When did you last feel nervous about something?
   b What do you feel confident about?
   c When was the last time you were delighted about something?
   d What kind of things make you angry?
   e What do you feel positive about for the future?

Writing Part 3

1 Read the writing task and the sample answer below and say which of a–c it answers.

Your English teacher has asked you to write a story. Your story must have this title:
   a The day I had a job interview.
   b The day I said the wrong thing.
   c The day I missed an exam.

Write your story in about 100 words.

> The day began badly. I heard a voice yelling up the stairs, 'Michael! It's 8.30! You've got an exam in an hour!' I jumped out of bed immediately and in ten minutes I had left the house and was running desperately to the bus stop. I arrived at college at 9.25 with five minutes left until the exam.
>
> I ran down the corridor and threw myself onto the chair in front of the examiner. 'Bonjour,' I said, slowly and calmly. The examiner looked at me and frowned. 'This is a Spanish exam, Michael, not a French exam. Would you like to start again?'

2 Read the answer again and find five adverbs.

tip You can make your writing more interesting by using adjectives and adverbs.

3 Read this answer to the same task in exercise 2, ignoring the gaps. Then complete it with suitable adverbs. Compare your answers with a partner.

I woke up, yawned (1).................. and looked at the clock. It was half past eight. I had a long shower and went downstairs. I ate my breakfast (2).................. , enjoying every mouthful, and thought about how much I loved weekends. (3).................. the phone rang. 'Alice!' a voice said (4).................. . 'Where are you?' 'I'm at home, of course,' I replied. 'But you've got a maths exam in half an hour!'

I slammed down the phone, picked up my bag and rushed out of the door. It was Friday, not Saturday! I ran as (5).................. as I could to the bus stop!

4 Choose one of the titles in exercise 1 and write your own answer.

Unit 14 107

4 Review Units 11–14

1 For questions 1–8 choose the correct answers.

1 one word that describes hot food such as curry
   a sweet   d bitter
   b salty   e fishy
   c spicy

2 two words that can describe chocolate
   a milk   b dark   c sour   d salty

3 two celebrations in December
   a Christmas Day   c New Year's Eve
   b New Year's Day   d Thanksgiving

4 three people traditionally at a wedding
   a commentator   d presenter
   b bride   e photographer
   c groom

5 three people that work in the media
   a cameraman   c paparazzi
   b journalist   d bridesmaid

6 three positive adjectives
   a confident   d miserable
   b delighted   e glad
   c frightened

7 two words related to rice
   a slice   b bar   c bowl   d packet

8 three negative adjectives
   a lonely   d excited
   b bored   e nervous
   c cheerful

2 Complete the phrasal verbs in sentences a–g.

a Please pick …… your clothes. They're lying all over the floor.
b We've run …… of sugar again. Can you buy some on your way home?
c Please turn …… the lights if you're the last person to leave the room.
d Don't turn …… the air conditioning! It isn't at all hot today!
e We asked our neighbour to cut …… their tree as it was growing into our garden.
f Let's go shopping. We need to fill …… the fridge. It's empty.
g You must give …… smoking. Don't you know how bad it is for you?

3 Read the text and for 1–10 choose the correct answer, A, B, C or D.

PROFILE OF A RAINFOREST VOLUNTEER

Max Hardy (1)……………… be a computer engineer. Then he gave up his well-paid job in order (2)……………… work as a volunteer in the Amazon rainforest. I asked Max why he (3)……………… this decision.

'I've always been interested in the environment,' he (4)……………… me. 'I know that if we don't (5)……………… something to change the situation, global warming will get worse.'

So what exactly does Max do in the rainforest?

'I'm living with a group of ten other volunteers, in a rainforest lodge,' he (6)……………… . 'We go out every day with our guide (7)……………… order to make notes about the birds, animals and plants. We give these details to scientists so (8)……………… they can see how life in the rainforest is changing.'

I asked Max (9)……………… there was anything he missed about home. 'I didn't (10)……………… to see my family very much, but I do really miss them.' Max also told me he missed eating hamburgers and chips!

108 Review 4

1 A use to   B used to   C use   D used
2 A for   B so   C to   D as
3 A had made   C will make
   B would make   D makes
4 A said   B asked   C told   D spoke
5 A do   B did   C have done
   D will do
6 A said   B told   C asked   D spoke
7 A for   B as   C in   D at
8 A which   B what   C where   D that
9 A unless   B when   C how   D if
10 A use   B used   C to use   D using

4 For a–h complete the second sentence so that it means the same as the first. Write no more than three words.

a 'Are you enjoying your course?' said Sam.
   Sam asked me if .... my course.

b Henry is the hardest worker in the class.
   No one in the class .... than Henry.

c Someone is fixing my bike at the moment.
   I .... my bike fixed at the moment.

d 'I'll see you next week!' said Lisa.
   Lisa said that she .... me the following week.

e I can't go shopping unless I finish my homework.
   If I finish my homework, ... shopping.

f I eat more healthily than anyone else in my family.
   Nobody in my family .... healthily as me.

g When I was a child, I didn't like school.
   I .... to like school when I was a child.

h Someone planted some trees in our garden last week.
   We .... planted in our garden last week.

5 Read the task and Claudia's letter, ignoring the mistakes, and find
a two punctuation mistakes
b four grammar mistakes

This is part of a letter you receive from your English pen friend, Suzie.

Now write a letter to Suzie, telling her about a party you went to. Write about 100 words.

I recently went to my friend's 18th birthday party. It was great fun. When did you last go to a good party? What was it for? What did you do and what did you enjoy most?

Hi Suzie

Thanks for your last letter. You told that you go to an 18th birthday party. It's sounding great!

I went to a really good party since two weeks. It was a surprise party for my parents' to celebrate their 25th wedding anniversary. We had a fantastic meal and afterwards there was music and dancing. The best bit for me was probably the food. I'm always loving eating! The worst bit was that we ran out off coke and I had to drink water.

I hope we can go to a party together one day.

Bye for now!

Love

Claudia

6 Write your own answer to the task in exercise 5.

Writing Guide

Part 2

- In Part 2 you have to write a short message of 35–45 words.
- The message could be a postcard, email, or note, etc.
- The rubric tells you who you are writing to and why, and what kind of message to write.
- The question gives you three points that you must include in your answer.
- Read the question carefully and make sure you know what you are writing and why.
- Plan your ideas for each of the three points.
- Start and end your message with a suitable phrase.
- Read through your answer and make sure you have included everything, and check for spelling, punctuation and grammar.
- Check the number of words you have written. If you don't include all three points, your answer may be too short. It may be too long if you include unnecessary information.

You are going on holiday. Write an email to your English friend, Pat. In your email you should

➡ say where you are going

➡ say what you plan to do

➡ suggest meeting after your holiday

Write 35–45 words.

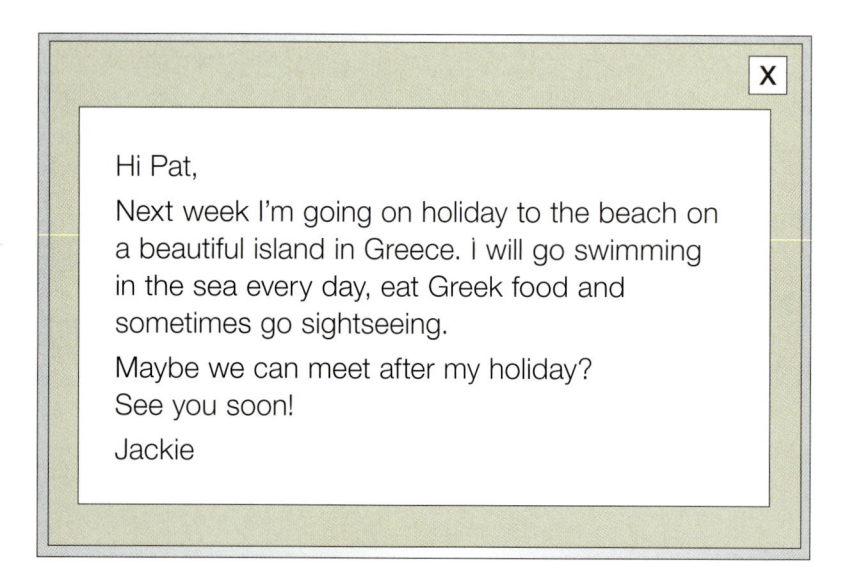

Hi Pat,

Next week I'm going on holiday to the beach on a beautiful island in Greece. i will go swimming in the sea every day, eat Greek food and sometimes go sightseeing.

Maybe we can meet after my holiday?
See you soon!

Jackie

Part 3

- In Part 3 you can choose to write either a story or an informal letter.
- Your answer must be about 100 words.
- For the informal letter you read part of a letter from a friend, which tells you what you must write.
- For the story the rubric gives you either the title or the first sentence of the story.
- Read both questions and decide quickly which one you prefer to answer.
- Think about the tenses you will need to use, and which adjectives and adverbs you can include to make your answer interesting.
- For the story, plan a beginning, middle and end before you start writing. Make sure your answer fits the title or the first sentence. Don't write a story you have memorised.
- For the letter, make a plan including everything the question asks for. Start and finish with suitable phrases.
- Read through your answer to check for spelling, punctuation and grammar. Make sure you have written the correct number of words.

This is part of a letter you receive from your English penfriend.

In your next letter, please tell me what you do in your free time.
What do you enjoy doing best? Who do you do it with?

Now write a letter answering your friend's questions.
Write about 100 words.

Dear Jim,

In your last letter you asked what I do in my free time. I have lots of hobbies. I like sports and I really enjoy playing tennis every Saturday with my brother. My favourite sport is basketball, so at the weekend I love watching American basketball games on TV with my best friend Dave.

Sometimes I go to the cinema with my friends. We especially enjoy seeing horror films because they are scary! However, my favourite kind of films are comedies because they make me laugh.

I also love listening to music and I often go to concerts.

Write to me soon,

Harry

Your English teacher has asked you to write a story.
Your story must have this title.
An exciting journey.

Write your story in about 100 words.

> An exciting journey
>
> It was summer and I was on holiday with my family. On the last day of the holiday, it was my birthday. My parents had a surprise for me – we took a boat trip from the island to see the dolphins.
>
> We got on the boat very early and sailed away from the coast. At first we didn't see any dolphins, so I was disappointed.
>
> We had lunch on the boat and everyone was singing 'Happy Birthday' when suddenly I saw dolphin fins! The dolphins were swimming and jumping next to the boat. It was the most exciting journey I've ever been on!

Audioscript

Listening 10 page 26

Harry	Hi Ella. How's university?
Ella	It's great thanks, Harry. I'm really enjoying it.
Harry	I imagine you're having a lot of fun and not studying at all!
Ella	You're right, I'm having a great time, but actually, doing history's really difficult. I write compositions, read loads of books and go to lectures. I often study late at night.
Harry	Oh, that's not so good then. What about clubs? Have you joined any?
Ella	I was in the photography club and the art club, but they used to meet too often and I didn't have time, so I left.
Harry	That's a real shame. I think I'll join the film club when I go to university.
Ella	Will that be next year?
Harry	Actually, I'm planning to have a year off before I start university. I feel I need a break from studying. I fancy going to South America to improve my Spanish.
Ella	Good idea, then you can go to university the year after and do a Spanish degree. You'll be much better than everybody else.
Harry	I love languages but I want to study them as a hobby. I'm hoping to do chemistry at university.
Ella	They do a good chemistry course at my university. Why don't you try there?
Harry	Thanks, but I'm considering applying to a few universities abroad.
Ella	Really? Where are you thinking of?
Harry	I've been looking at universities in the US or maybe in Canada.
Ella	What about Spain?
Harry	Well, my Spanish is good, but it isn't that good. I couldn't study chemistry in Spanish at the moment.
Ella	After a year in South America you might be able to!
Harry	I don't think so.
Ella	Well, I'm sure wherever you go you'll have a great time!
Harry	Thanks! I'm sure I will too!

Writing Guide

Vocabulary Reference

Unit 1

Holidays
abroad
accommodation
backpack
baggage
brochure
camp(ing)
campsite
capital city
cruise (ship)
facilities
foreign
guest(house)
guide(book)
hotel
immigration
luggage
on holiday / vacation
reserve / reservation
safari
sightseeing
suitcase
sunbathing
tent
tour(ist)
trip
villa
visa
visit(or)
youth hostel

Travel and transport
(aero)plane
(bi)cycle / bike
(bus) service
airline
airport
board (v)
boarding pass
boat
bus (station / stop)
by air / land / rail / road / sea
cab
cabin
car
catch
change
check in / out (v)
check-in (n)
coach
customs (officer)
cyclist
deck (of ship)
depart(ure)
destination
document
drive
driving licence
fare
ferry
flight
fly
fuel
gate
handlebars
helicopter
hot-air balloon
hovercraft
jet
journey
land
lorry
motorbike / motorcycle
motorway
on board
on foot
passenger
passport
pilot
platform
railway
sail
scooter
ship
take off
taxi (rank)
terminal
traffic (jam / lights)
train
tram
underground
vehicle
voyage

Countryside
bay
beach
canal
cliff
coast
desert
earth
farm
field
forest
harbour
hill
island
lake
land
mountain
ocean
rainforest
region
river
rock
sand
scenery
sea(side)
stream
valley
village
waterfall
wood

Unit 2

Hobbies and leisure
archaeology
camera
chess
club
collect(or) / collection
computer
cookery
dancing
drama
drawing
dressmaking
fiction
keep fit
gallery
guitar
jogging
join in
keen on
member(ship)
model
museum
music
paint(ing)
photography
playing cards
wildlife

Education
arithmetic
art
biology
certificate
chemistry
class(room)
coach
college
composition
course
curriculum
degree

Vocabulary Reference 113

desk
diploma
economics
educate / education
essay
geography
history
handwriting
homework
instructor
IT
laboratory
language
learn(er)
lecture(r)
lesson
mark
mathematics / maths
music
physics
primary school
professor
pupil
qualify / qualification
register
revise
science
secondary school
state school
subject
study
technology
undergraduate
university

Unit 3
Shopping
bargain
buy
cash
change
cheap
cheque
complain
cost (n and v)
credit card
dear
deposit
(at a) discount
exchange
(in)expensive
hire
luxury
money
order
pay
price
reasonable
receipt
reduce(d)
reserve
return
sale(s)
save
sell

Clothes
blouse
boot
bra
casual
coat
collar
cotton
dress
elegant
fashionable
fasten
fit (v)
formal
get dressed
go with
jacket
jeans
jumper
leather
match
material
old-fashioned
pants
pattern
plastic
pocket
pullover
put on
pyjamas
raincoat
shirt
shoe
shorts
silk
size
skirt
sleeve(less)
smart
sock
stockings
suit
sweater
sweatshirt
swimming costume
swimsuit
T-shirt
take off
tie
tights
tracksuit
trainers
trousers
try on
underwear
wear (out)
wool(len)

Accessories
belt
bracelet
earring
glove
hat
glasses
handbag
handkerchief
jewellery
necklace
scarf

Unit 4
Animal parts
beak
claw
feather
fin
fur
hair
hoof
paw
skin
tail
tooth
wing

Animals
bird
cat
chimpanzee
dog
dolphin
duck
elephant
fish
giraffe
horse
insect
kitten
lion
monkey
mouse / mice
puppy
rabbit
shark
snake
spider
tail
tiger
whale
zebra

Parts of the body
ankle
arm
chest
ear

elbow
eye
finger
foot
hair
hand
head
knee
leg
mouth
nail
neck
nose
shoulder
skin
stomach
thumb
toe
tooth / teeth
waist
wrist

Films
act(ion)
actor / actress
adventure
animation
cartoon
cinema
comedy / comedian
costume
documentary
drama
fantasy
film (maker / star)
(computer) graphics
hero / heroine
historical (drama)
horror
romantic
scene
science fiction
screen
special effects
star
thriller
western

Unit 5
Health and sport
ache
cut down on
diet
feel better / ill / sick
fit(ness)
get better / worse
give up
hurt
injure
keep fit
medicine
recover
stress
take exercise
take up

Sports
athlete / athletics
baseball
basketball
bat
boxing
champion
coach (n and v)
diving
football
goal
golf
gym(nastics)
helmet
hit (n and v)
(ice) hockey
horse riding
ice skating
jogging
judo
kick (n and v)
mask
match
motor racing
net
player
practice / practise
racket
referee
riding
rugby
running
sail(ing)
score
scuba-diving
skiing
squash
stick (n)
surfing
swimming
table-tennis
take part (in)
tennis
tracksuit
train(ing)
volleyball
water skiing

Sports places
court
pitch
stadium
track

Unit 6
Places to live
apartment (block)
bungalow
castle
city (centre)
cottage
(block of) flats
palace
town (centre)
village

Parts of a home
balcony
basement
bathroom
bedroom
ceiling
cellar
chimney
corridor
dining room
fence
garage
gate
ground (floor)
hall
kitchen
lavatory / toilet / WC
living room
lounge
patio
roof
shower
sitting room
stairs
study

Unit 7
Entertainment
audience
ballet
band
circus
comedy / comedian
concert
costume
dance
drama
entrance
exhibition
exit
festival
(classical / jazz / rock / folk) music
interval
opera
orchestra
performance
play
poem
review
scene
stage
star

Unit 8
Things in the home
air-conditioning
armchair
basin
blanket
bookshelf
carpet
chest of drawers
cooker
cupboard
curtain
cushion
dish(washer)
dustbin
fan
fork
freezer
fridge
frying pan
furniture
handle
iron
jug
kettle
knife
lamp
microwave (n)
mug
oven
pan
pillow
plate
refrigerator
saucepan
shelf
sink
spoon
table(cloth)
tap
towel
vase
washbasin
washing machine
wastepaper basket

Weather
blizzard
boiling
centigrade
cloud(y)
cool
cold
degrees
drought
dry
flood
forecast
frost
fog(gy)
freezing
gale
hail
heat
hot
humid
hurricane
ice / icy
lightning
mild
rain(y)
shower
snow(y)
snowfall
storm(y)
sun(ny) / sunshine
temperature
thermometer
thunder(storm)
tornado
wet
wind(y)

Unit 9
Technology
calculator
CD / CD-Rom / CD player
computer
connect(ion)
digital
disc / disk
DVD (player)
electronic(s)
email
equipment
(the) Internet
invent(ion)
IT
keyboard
laptop
laser
machine
mobile phone
mouse (mat)
network
online
print(er)
program(me)
screen
software
switch on / off
turn on / off

Work and jobs
architect
artist
athlete
banker
businessman / businesswoman
butcher
cameraman
captain
carpenter
chef
chemist
clerk
cook
dancer
dentist
designer
detective
director
disc jockey
diver
doctor
engineer
farmer
fireman
(green)grocer
hairdresser
instructor
interpreter
journalist
judge
lawyer
lecturer
librarian
manager
mechanic
model
musician
novelist
nurse
officer
photographer
pilot
policeman / policewoman / police officer
politician
postman
presenter
producer
reporter
sailor
salesman / saleswoman
scientist
secretary
shop assistant
soldier
taxi driver
teacher
waiter / waitress
writer

Unit 10
Family members
aunt
brother
child
cousin
daughter
father
grandchild / daughter / father / mother / parent / son
mother
nephew
niece

116 Vocabulary Reference

sister
son
uncle

Personality adjectives
bossy
brave
clever
cowardly
cruel
funny
generous
gentle
hard-working
intelligent
jealous
keen
kind
lazy
lucky
patient
pleasant
polite
positive
punctual
realistic
reliable
rude
selfish
serious
smart
sociable
stupid

Unit 11
The natural world
bottle bank
climate (change)
continent
earth
environment
land
litter
petrol
planet
plant
pollution
rainforest

rock
sand
scenery
sky
soil
wild(life)

Unit 12
Food and drink
apple
banana
bar
biscuit
bitter
bowl
bread
butter
can
carrot
cereal
cheese
chicken
cup
curry
dessert
dish
fish(y)
fruit (juice)
grape
hot
lemon
menu
milk
nut
oil
onion
orange
packet
pasta
pastry
pea
raisin
recipe
rice
salt(y)
slice
sour

spicy
spoonful
sugar
sweet
vegetable
vegetarian

Ways of cooking
bake
barbecue
boil
fry
grill
roast

Unit 13
TV and media
advert / advertisement
cameraman
channel
chat show
commentator
DJ (disc jockey)
documentary
editor
journalist
magazine
news(paper)
paparazzi
photographer
presenter
programme
quiz
reality TV
reporter
series
soap opera
studio
television
weather forecast

Unit 14
Communicating
address
by post
call
chat
communicate / communication
email
message
parcel
postcard
ring up
(tele)phone
text (message)

Personal feelings
angry
annoyed
anxious
ashamed
bored
cheerful
confident
curious
delighted
depressed
disappointed
embarrassed
excited
frightened
glad
guilty
happy
jealous
keen
lonely
miserable
nervous
positive
reasonable
realistic
relaxed
sad
satisfied
serious
surprised
tired

Grammar Reference

Irregular verbs

Infinitive	Past tense	Past participle
arise	arose	arisen
awake	awoke	awoken
be	was/were	been
bear	bore	borne
beat	beat	beaten
become	became	become
begin	began	begun
bend	bent	bent
bet	bet, betted	bet, betted
bid	bid	bid
bind	bound	bound
bite	bit	bitten
bleed	bled	bled
blow	blew	blown
break	broke	broken
breed	bred	bred
bring	brought	brought
broadcast	broadcast	broadcast
build	built	built
burn	burnt, burned	burnt, burned
burst	burst	burst
bust	bust, busted	bust, busted
buy	bought	bought
cast	cast	cast
catch	caught	caught
choose	chose	chosen
cling	clung	clung
come	came	come
cost	cost	cost
creep	crept	crept
cut	cut	cut
deal	dealt	dealt
dig	dug	dug
dive	dived	dived
do	did	done
draw	drew	drawn
dream	dreamt, dreamed	dreamt, dreamed
drink	drank	drunk
drive	drove	driven
eat	ate	eaten
fall	fell	fallen
feed	fed	fed
feel	felt	felt

Infinitive	Past tense	Past participle
fight	fought	fought
find	found	found
flee	fled	fled
fling	flung	flung
fly	flew	flown
forbid	forbade, forbad	forbidden
forecast	forecast	forecast
foresee	foresaw	foreseen
forget	forgot	forgotten
forgive	forgave	forgiven
forgo	forwent	forgone
forsake	forsook	forsaken
freeze	froze	frozen
get	got	got; (US) gotten
give	gave	given
go	went	gone
grind	ground	ground
grow	grew	grown
hang	hung, hanged	hung, hanged
have	had	had
hear	heard	heard
hide	hid	hidden
hit	hit	hit
hold	held	held
hurt	hurt	hurt
keep	kept	kept
kneel	knelt; (esp US) kneeled	knelt; (esp US) kneeled
know	knew	known
lay	laid	laid
lead	led	led
lean	leant, leaned	leant, leaned
leap	leapt, leaped	leapt, leaped
learn	learnt, learned	learnt, learned
leave	left	left
lend	lent	lent
let	let	let
lie	lay	lain

Infinitive	Past tense	Past participle
light	lighted, lit	lighted, lit
lose	lost	lost
make	made	made
mean	meant	meant
meet	met	met
mislay	mislaid	mislaid
mislead	misled	misled
misread	misread	misread
misspell	misspelt, misspelled	misspelt, misspelled
mistake	mistook	mistaken
outdo	outdid	outdone
outgrow	outgrew	outgrown
overcome	overcame	overcome
overdo	overdid	overdone
overhear	overheard	overheard
overpay	overpaid	overpaid
override	overrode	overridden
overrun	overran	overrun
oversee	oversaw	overseen
oversleep	overslept	overslept
overtake	overtook	overtaken
overthrow	overthrew	overthrown
pay	paid	paid
prove	proved	proved
put	put	put
quit	quit	quit
read	read	read
rebuild	rebuilt	rebuilt
repay	repaid	repaid
rethink	rethought	rethought
rewrite	rewrote	rewritten
rid	rid	rid
ride	rode	ridden
ring	rang	rung
rise	rose	risen
run	ran	run
saw	sawed	sawn
say	said	said
see	saw	seen
seek	sought	sought
sell	sold	sold
send	sent	sent
set	set	set
sew	sewed	sewn, sewed

Infinitive	Past tense	Past participle
shake	shook	shaken
shed	shed	shed
shine	shone	shone
shoe	shod	shod
shoot	shot	shot
show	showed	shown, showed
shrink	shrank, shrunk	shrunk
shut	shut	shut
sing	sang	sung
sink	sank	sunk
sit	sat	sat
slay	slew	slain
sleep	slept	slept
slide	slid	slid
sling	slung	slung
slink	slunk	slunk
slit	slit	slit
smell	smelt, smelled	smelt, smelled
sow	sowed	sown, sowed
speak	spoke	spoken
speed	sped, speeded	sped, speeded
spell	spelt, spelled	spelt, spelled
spend	spent	spent
spill	spilt, spilled	spilt, spilled
spin	spun	spun
spit	spat	spat
split	split	split
spoil	spoilt, spoiled	spoilt, spoiled
spread	spread	spread
spring	sprang	sprung
stand	stood	stood
steal	stole	stolen
stick	stuck	stuck
sting	stung	stung
stink	stank, stunk	stunk
stride	strode	—
strike	struck	struck
string	strung	strung
strive	strove	striven
swear	swore	sworn
sweep	swept	swept
swell	swelled	swollen, swelled
swim	swam	swum
swing	swung	swung
take	took	taken
teach	taught	taught

Infinitive	Past tense	Past participle
tear	tore	torn
tell	told	told
think	thought	thought
throw	threw	thrown
thrust	thrust	thrust
tread	trod	trodden
understand	understood	understood
undo	undid	undone
upset	upset	upset
wake	woke	woken
wear	wore	worn
weep	wept	wept
wet	wet, wetted	wet, wetted
win	won	won
wind	wound	wound
withdraw	withdrew	withdrawn
withhold	withheld	withheld
write	wrote	written

Be, do, have

Full forms	Short forms	Negative short forms
be present tense		
I am	I'm	I'm not
you are	you're	you're not/you aren't
he is	he's	he's not/he isn't
she is	she's	she's not/she isn't
it is	it's	it's not/it isn't
we are	we're	we're not/we aren't
you are	you're	you're not/you aren't
they are	they're	they're not/they aren't
be past tense		
I was	—	I wasn't
you were	—	you weren't
he was	—	he wasn't
she was	—	she wasn't
it was	—	it wasn't
we were	—	we weren't
you were	—	you weren't
they were	—	they weren't
have present tense		
I have	I've	I haven't/I've not
you have	you've	you haven't/you've not
he has	he's	he hasn't/he's not
she has	she's	she hasn't/she's not
it has	it's	it hasn't/it's not
we have	we've	we haven't/we've not
you have	you've	you haven't/you've not
they have	they've	they haven't/they've not

have past tense (all persons)
had	I'd	hadn't
	you'd	
	etc.	

do present tense
I do	—	I don't
you do	—	you don't
he does	—	he doesn't
she does	—	she doesn't
it does	—	it doesn't
we do	—	we don't
you do	—	you don't
they do	—	they don't

do past tense (all persons)
| did | — | didn't |

	be	do	have
present participle	being	doing	having
past participle	been	done	had

- The negative full forms are formed by adding **not**.
- Questions in the present and past are formed by placing the verb before the subject:
  ▸ *am I?*   *isn't he?*
     was I?   *weren't we?*
     do I?   *didn't I?*
     have I?   *hadn't they?*
     etc.

Auxiliary verbs

- **Do** is used to form questions and negatives in the present and past simple. Note that the auxiliary verb and not the main verb shows the negative past tense:
  ▸ *She washed.*
  ▸ *She didn't wash.*
- **Have** is used to form the perfect tenses:
  ▸ *I haven't finished.*
  ▸ *Has he arrived yet?*
  ▸ *They hadn't seen each other for a long time.*
- **Be** is used to form the continuous tenses and the passive:
  ▸ *I'm studying Italian.*
  ▸ *We were watching TV.*
  ▸ *It was painted by a famous artist.*

Verbs

Regular verbs: the simple tenses

Present simple

I/we/you/they work	do not work (don't work)	Do **I** work?
he/she/it works	does not work (doesn't work)	Does **he** work?

Past simple

I/we/you/they/he/she/it worked — did not work (didn't work) — Did **they** work?

Future simple

I/we/you/they/he/she/it will work (**he'll** work) — will not work (won't work) — Will **he** work?

Present perfect

I/we/you/they have worked (**I've** worked) — have not worked (haven't worked) — Have **you** worked?

he/she/it has worked (**she's** worked) — has not worked (hasn't worked) — Has **she** worked?

Past perfect

I/we/you/they/he/she/it had worked (**they'd** worked) — had not worked (hadn't worked) — Had **they** worked?

Conditional

I/we/you/they/he/she/it would work (**I'd** work) — would not work (wouldn't work) — Would **you** work?

Regular verbs: the continuous tenses

NOTE The continuous tenses are sometimes called the progressive tenses.

Present continuous

I am working (**I'm** working) — am not working (**I'm** not working) — Am **I** working?

you/we/they are working (**you're** working) — are not working (aren't working) — Are **you** working?

he/she/it is working (**he's** working) — is not working (isn't working) — Is **he** working?

Past continuous

I/he/she/it was working — was not working (wasn't working) — Was **he** working?

we/you/they were working — were not working (weren't working) — Were **you** working?

Future continuous

I/we/you/they/he/she/it will be working (**he'll** be working) — will not be working (won't be working) — Will **he** be working?

Grammar Reference

Talking about the present

You use the **present continuous**

- to talk about an action that is happening now:
  - ▸ *We're waiting for a train.*
  - ▸ *What are you doing?*
  - ▸ *She's listening to the radio.*

- to talk about something that is not yet finished, even if you are not doing it at the moment when you are talking:
  - ▸ *I'm learning the guitar.*
  - ▸ *He's writing a book about fashion.*

- with **always**, to talk about something that happens often, and that you find annoying:
  - ▸ *He's always asking to borrow money.*
  - ▸ *She's always phoning her friends late at night.*

  NOTE Some verbs are not used in the continuous tenses, for example **need**, **want**, **know**, **hear**, **smell**, **agree**, **seem**, **appear**, **understand**, etc. These verbs refer to a state, not an action:
  - ▸ *I need a holiday.*
  - ▸ *She hates the new house.*
  - ▸ *They love Indian food.*
  - ▸ *He wants to be alone.*
  - ▸ *Do you know Lucy Johnston?*

  Other verbs are used in the present continuous when they refer to an action, and the present simple when they refer to a state:
  - ▸ *She's tasting the cheese.*
  - ▸ *The cheese tastes salty.*
  - ▸ *He's being noisy today.*
  - ▸ *He's a noisy dog.*
  - ▸ *What are you thinking about?*
  - ▸ *Do you think I should leave?*

You use the **present simple**

- to talk about a permanent situation:
  - ▸ *He lives in Scotland.*
  - ▸ *She works in local government.*

- to talk about something that is always true:
  - ▸ *Oranges don't grow this far north.*
  - ▸ *What temperature does water freeze at?*

- to talk about things that happen regularly:
  - ▸ *She goes to yoga every Monday.*
  - ▸ *We don't often go to the theatre.*

Talking about the past

You use the **past simple**

- to talk about an action that took place in the past:
  - ▸ *He turned round, dropped the bag and ran away.*
  - ▸ *I didn't write to her, but I rang her.*
  - ▸ *Where did you stay in Glasgow?*

  NOTE Often a specific time is mentioned:
  - ▸ *Did you see Rory yesterday?*

- to talk about a state that continued for some time, but that is now finished:
  - ▸ *I went to school in Ireland.*
  - ▸ *Did she really work there for ten years?*

- to talk about actions that happened regularly in the past:
  - ▸ *They often played chess together. She always won.*
  - ▸ *We always went to Devon for our summer holidays when I was a child.*

You can also **used to** for actions that happened regularly or continued for some time in the past:
- ▸ *I used to like chocolate, but I don't eat it now.*
- ▸ *Did you use to live in Australia?*

You use the **present perfect**

- to talk about something that happened during a period of time that is not yet finished:
  - ▸ *The train has been late three times this week.*
  - ▸ *He still hasn't visited her.*

- when the time is not mentioned, or is not important:
  - ▸ *He's written a book.*
    (BUT *He wrote a book last year.*)
  - ▸ *I've bought a bike.*
    (BUT *I bought a bike on Saturday.*)

- when the action finished in the past, but the effect is still felt in the present:
  - ▸ *He's lost his wallet*
    (and he still hasn't found it).

- with **for** and **since** to show the duration of an action or state up until the present:
  - ▸ *She hasn't bought any new clothes for ages.*
  - ▸ *They have lived here for ten years, and they don't want to move.*
  - ▸ *I've worked here since 1998.*

- in British English with **just**, **ever**, **already** and **yet**:
  - ▸ *I've just arrived.*
  - ▸ *Have you ever been here before?*
  - ▸ *He's already packed his suitcases.*
  - ▸ *Haven't you finished yet?*

You use the **past continuous**

- to talk about something that was already in progress when something else happened:
  - ▸ *The telephone rang while we were having dinner.*
  - ▸ *Was it raining when you left the house?*

  NOTE As with the present continuous, this tense cannot be used with 'state' verbs:
  - ▸ *Jamie's cake tasted delicious.*
    (NOT *was tasting*)

You use the **past perfect**

- to talk about something that happened before another action in the past:
  - ▸ *When I got to the airport, the plane had already left.*
  - ▸ *They had just bought a flat when Joe lost his job.*

You use the **past perfect continuous**

- to talk about an activity that went on for a period of time further back in the past than something else:
  - ▸ *My hands were dirty because I had been digging the garden.*
  - ▸ *She hadn't been working at the shop very long when they sacked her.*

Talking about the future

There are several ways of talking about the future.

You use **be going to** with the **infinitive**

- to talk about what you intend to do in the future:
  - ▸ *I'm going to see a film tonight.*
  - ▸ *What are you going to do when you leave school?*

- to make predictions based on a present situation:
  - ▸ *It's almost 10am. We're going to miss the train.*

You use the **future simple**
(**will** with the infinitive)

- to talk about a decision that you make as you are speaking:
  - ▸ *It's warm in here. I'll open a window.*

Grammar Reference

▶ *I'll have* the salad, please.

- to talk about what you know or think will happen in the future (but not about your own intentions or plans):
  ▶ *She'll be* 25 on her next birthday.
  ▶ *Will* he *pass* the exam, do you think?
  ▶ This job *won't take* long.

- for requests, promises, and offers:
  ▶ *Will* you *buy* some milk on your way home?
  ▶ *We'll be* back soon, don't worry.
  ▶ *I'll help* you with your homework.

You use the **present continuous**

- to talk about future plans where the time is mentioned:
  ▶ *He's flying* to Thailand in June.
  ▶ What *are* you *doing* this weekend?
  ▶ *I'm not starting* my new job till next Monday.

You use the **present simple**

- to talk about future plans where something has been officially arranged, for example on a timetable or programme:
  ▶ We *leave* Prague at 10 and *arrive* in London at 11.50.
  ▶ School *starts* on 3rd September.

- to refer to a future time after when, as soon as, before, until, etc.:
  ▶ Ring me as soon as you *hear* any news.
  ▶ I'll look after Tim until you *get* back.
  ▶ You'll remember Dita when you *see* her.

Conditionals

Sentences with *if* express possibilities.

something that is always true or was always true in the past (zero conditional):
  ▶ If you *pour* oil on water, it *floats*.

Present simple in both parts of the sentence.

(first conditional) possible – it might happen in the future:
  ▶ If I *win* £100, I *will take* you to Paris.
  ▶ If I *pass* the exam, I'll *go* to medical school.

Present tense after *if*, **future tense** in the main clause.

(second conditional) improbable – it is unlikely to happen in the future:
  ▶ If I *won* £100, I *would take* you to Paris.
  ▶ If I *passed* the exam, I *would go* to medical school.

Past simple after *if*, **conditional tense** in the main clause.

Modal verbs

Ability

can • could • be able to

▶ *Can* he swim?
▶ My sister *could* read when she was four.
▶ I *couldn't* find my shoes this morning.
▶ I *could have* run faster, but I didn't want to get tired.
▶ She *has* not *been able to* walk since the accident.
▶ He *was able to* speak to Tracey before she left.
▶ Will people *be able to* live on the moon one day?

Possibility

could • may • might • can

▶ *Could/Might* you have left it on the bus?
▶ She *may/might/could* be ill. I'll phone her.
▶ I *may have/might have* left my purse in the shop.
▶ Liz *might/may* know where it is.
▶ I *might/may* not go if I'm tired.
▶ He *might have* enjoyed the party if he'd gone.
▶ His wife *can* be very difficult at times.

Permission

can • could • may

▶ *Can* we come in?
▶ *Could* we possibly stay at your flat?
▶ Staff *may* take their break between 12 and 2. (formal)
▶ *May* I sit here? (formal)

Prohibition

cannot • may not • must not

▶ You *can't* get up until you're better.
▶ You *mustn't* tell anyone I'm here.
▶ Crockery *may not* be taken out of the canteen. (written)
▶ You *must not* begin until I tell you. (formal)

Obligation

have (got) to • must

▶ All visitors *must* report to reception on arrival.
▶ I *must* get that letter written today.
▶ Do you *have to* write your age on the form?
▶ She *had to* wait an hour for the bus.
▶ You *will have to* ring back later, I'm afraid.

Advice and criticism

ought to • should

▶ *Ought I to/Should* I wear a jacket?
▶ She *ought to/should* get her hair cut.
▶ You *ought to/should have* gone to bed earlier.
▶ You *ought not to/shouldn't* borrow the car without asking.
▶ I *ought to/should* go on a diet.
▶ I *ought to have/should have* asked her first.

No necessity

don't have to • shouldn't have •
didn't need to • needn't have

▶ You *don't have to* cook, we can get a takeaway.
▶ They *didn't have to* show their passports.
▶ You *shouldn't have* bought me a present.
▶ He *didn't need to* have any fillings at the dentist's.
▶ They *needn't have* waited.

Requests

can • could • will • would

▶ *Can* you help me lift this box?
▶ *Could* you pass me the salt?
▶ *Will* you buy me a puppy, Dad?
▶ *Would* you post this letter for me, please?

Could and **would** are more formal than **can** and **will**.

Offers and suggestions

shall • will • can

▶ *Shall* I make you a sandwich?
▶ *I'll (I will)* drive you to the station.
▶ *Shall* we go now?
▶ *Can* I help you?

122 Grammar Reference

The passive

In an active sentence, the subject is the person or thing that performs the action:
▸ *Masked thieves* stole a valuable painting from the museum last night.

When you make this into a passive sentence the object of the verb becomes the subject:
▸ *A valuable painting* was stolen from the museum last night.

The passive is made with the auxiliary verb **to be** and the **past participle** of the verb:

present simple	The painting **is valued** by experts at 2 million dollars.
present continuous	The theft **is being investigated** by the police.
present perfect	Other museums **have been warned** to take extra care.
past simple	The painting **was kept** in a special room.
past perfect	The lock **had been broken**.
past continuous	This morning everything possible **was being done** to find the thieves.
future	Staff at the museum **will be questioned** tomorrow.

You use the **passive**

- when you want to save new information until the end of the sentence for emphasis:
  ▸ The picture **was painted** by Turner.
- when you do not know who performed the action, or when this information is not important. It is common in formal writing, for example scientific writing:
  ▸ The liquid **is heated** to 60° and then filtered.

If you want to say who performed the action, you use **by** at the end of the sentence:
▸ The painting was stolen **by** masked thieves.

It is possible to put a verb that has two objects into the passive:
▸ An American millionaire gave the museum the painting.
▸ The museum **was given** the painting by an American millionaire.

have / get something done

You use *have / get something done* with a passive sense, meaning that the subject arranges for someone else to do the action:
▸ She **had** her house **decorated** last year.
▸ Where **do** you **get** your hair **cut**?

Reported speech

Reported (or indirect) speech is the term used for the words that are used to report what someone has said.

If the reporting verb (say, ask, etc.) is in the present or present perfect, then the tense of the sentence does not change:
▸ 'I'm going home.'
▸ Bob says he's going home.
▸ Bob's just told me he's going home.

Reporting statements in the past

When you report somebody's words using said, asked, etc., you usually change the tense to one further back in the past:

present simple	I **don't know** whether Nell **wants** an ice cream.'
past simple	He said he **didn't know** whether Nell **wanted** an ice cream.
present continuous	'She **is hoping** to rent a car tomorrow.'
past continuous	He said she **was hoping** to rent a car the following day.
present perfect	'**Have** you **brought** your licence?'
past perfect	He asked whether she **had brought** her licence.
past simple	'I **passed** my driving test yesterday.'
past perfect	He said he **had passed** his driving test the day before.
will	'I'**ll ring** from the airport.'
would	She told me she **would ring** from the airport.
can	'I **can play** the flute.'
could	He said he **could play** the flute.

- Other changes:
  I/you/we becomes **he/she/they**, my/your becomes **his/her**, etc.
- Time references change:
  tomorrow becomes **the following day**, **yesterday** becomes the **day before**, **last week** becomes **the week before/ the previous week**, etc.
- The modal verbs **should**, **would**, **might**, **could**, **must**, and **ought to** are not usually changed:
  ▸ 'We **might** get a dog.'
  ▸ They said they **might** get a dog.

Reporting requests and commands

When you report a request or an order, you usually use a to-infinitive:
▸ 'Please will you wash the dishes?'
▸ She asked me **to wash** the dishes.
▸ 'Don't eat all the cake!'
▸ She told the children **not to eat** all the cake.

Reporting questions

Notice that you use **if** or **whether** to report yes/no questions:
▸ 'Are you ready?'
▸ She asked **if/whether** I was ready.

With **wh-** questions, the **wh-** word stays in the sentence:
▸ 'When are you leaving?'
▸ She asked me **when** I was leaving.

The word order in these sentences is the same as a normal statement, not as in a question:
▸ 'Did you see them?'
▸ He asked me if I had seen them.

Verb patterns

When one verb is followed by another, you need to know what form the second verb should take. The meaning of the verb can sometimes make one pattern more likely than another. The following points can help you to make a good guess:

Many verbs that suggest that **an action will follow, or will be completed successfully**, are followed by **to do**:

(can) afford to do sth
agree to do sth
decide to do sth
hope to do sth
intend to do sth
offer to do sth
plan to do sth
manage to do sth
remember to do sth
try to do sth (or try doing sth)
volunteer to do sth
ask (sb) to do sth

Grammar Reference 123

expect (sb) to do sth
help (sb) to do sth
need (sb) to do sth
wait (for sb) to do sth
want (sb) to do sth
would like (sb) to do sth
advise sb to do sth
allow sb to do sth
encourage sb to do sth
enable sb to do sth
get sb to do sth
persuade sb to do sth
remind sb to do sth
teach sb to do sth
tell sb to do sth

But note these verbs, which have a similar meaning but a different pattern:

let sb do sth
make sb do sth
consider doing sth
think about doing sth
suggest doing sth
recommend doing sth
look forward to doing sth
succeed in doing sth

Several verbs that suggest that **an action is unlikely to follow, or to be completed successfully**, are followed by an **-ing** form, sometimes with a preposition too:

avoid doing sth
resist doing sth
put sb off doing sth
save sb (from) doing sth
prevent sb from doing sth
advise sb against doing sth
  (or *advise sb not to do sth*)

But note these verbs:

forget to do sth
fail to do sth
refuse to do sth

Several verbs that refer to **past events or actions** are followed by an **-ing** form, sometimes with a preposition:

admit doing sth
celebrate doing sth
miss doing sth
remember doing sth
regret doing sth
thank sb for doing sth

Verbs that refer to **starting**, **stopping** or **continuing** are often followed by an **-ing** form:

begin doing sth
continue doing sth
carry on doing sth
finish doing sth
put off doing sth
go on doing sth
start doing sth

But note that you can also say:

begin to do sth
continue to do sth
start to do sth

Verbs meaning **like and dislike** are usually followed by an **-ing** form:

like doing sth
love doing sth
prefer doing sth
hate doing sth
dread doing sth

But note that you can also say:

hate to do sth
like to do sth
prefer to do sth

Phrasal verbs

Phrasal verbs are verbs that have two parts – a **verb** (sit, give, look, get, etc.) and a **particle** (down, up, after, etc.). Some phrasal verbs (come down with, put up with, etc.) have two particles.

sit down	give up
look after	get along with

Many phrasal verbs are easy to understand. For example, if you know the words **sit** and **down**, you can guess the meaning of **sit down**. But some phrasal verbs are more difficult because they have special meanings. For example, "**give up** smoking" means "stop smoking", but you can't guess this, even if you know the words **give** and **up**.

The four types

There are four main types of phrasal verb:
Type 1
Phrasal verbs without an object
▶ *Please **sit down**.*
▶ *I have to **get up** early tomorrow.*

In the dictionary, these verbs are written like this: **sit down**; **get up**.

Type 2
Phrasal verbs that can be separated by an object

If the object is a noun, it can go either *after* both parts of the phrasal verb or *between* them:
▶ *She **tried on** the red sweater.*
▶ *She **tried** the red sweater **on**.*

If the object is a pronoun, it must go between the two parts of the phrasal verb:
▶ *She **tried** it **on**.* (NOT *She tried on it.*)

In the dictionary, this verb is written like this: **try sth on**. When you see **sth** or **sb** between the two parts of the phrasal verb, you know that they can be separated by an object.

Type 3
Phrasal verbs that cannot be separated by an object

The two parts of the phrasal verb must go together:
▶ *Could you **look after** my dog while I'm on holiday?* (NOT *Could you look my dog after while I'm on holiday?*)
▶ *Could you **look after** it while I'm on holiday?* (NOT *Could you look it after while I'm on holiday?*)

Type 4
Phrasal verbs with three parts

The three parts of the phrasal verb must go together:
▶ *I can't **put up with** this noise anymore.*

Nouns

Countable and uncountable nouns

[C]
Countable nouns can be singular or plural:
▶ *a friend/two friends*
▶ *one book/five books*

[U]
Uncountable nouns cannot have a plural and are not used with **a/an**. They cannot be counted. It is possible to say **some rice** but not **a rice** or **two rices**.

Abstract nouns like **importance**, **luck**, **happiness** are usually uncountable.

[C,U]

Some nouns have both countable and uncountable meanings.

cheese   coffee   paper   friendship

- [U] *Have some cheese!*
- [C] *They sell a variety of cheeses.*
   (= types of cheese)
- [U] *I don't drink much coffee.*
- [C] *She ordered two coffees.*
   (= cups of coffee)
- [U] *I haven't got any more paper.*
- [C] *Can you buy me a paper?*
   (= a newspaper)
- [U] *Friendship is more important than wealth.*
- [C] *None of these were lasting friendships.* (= relationships)

[sing]

Some nouns are only singular. They cannot be used in the plural.

the countryside   the doctor's   a laugh

- *We love walking in the countryside.*
- *I'm going to the doctor's today.*
- *The party was a good laugh.*

[pl]

Other words are only plural.

jeans   sunglasses   scissors

You cannot say *a sunglasses*. To talk about individual items, you say **a pair**:

- *a pair of sunglasses*
- *two pairs of sunglasses*

Words like **headphones**, **clothes**, and **goods** can only be used in the plural:

- *I need to buy some new clothes.*

Nouns which describe groups of people, such as **the poor** are plural:

- *The poor are getting poorer and the rich are getting richer.*

Articles

The definite article

You use the definite article, **the**, when you expect the person who is listening to know which person or thing you are talking about:

- *Thank you for the flowers*
   (= the ones that you brought me).
- *The teacher said my essay was the best*
   (= our teacher).

You use **the** with the names of rivers and groups of islands:

- *Which is longer, the Rhine or the Danube?*
- *Where are the Seychelles?*
- *Menorca is one of the Balearic Islands.*

The indefinite article

You use the indefinite article, **a** (**an** before a vowel sound), when the other person does not know which person or thing you are talking about or when you are not referring to a particular thing or person:

- *He's got a new bike.*
   (I haven't mentioned it before.)
- *Can I borrow a pen?*
   (Any pen will be okay.)

You also use **a/an** to talk about a type or class of people or things, such as when you describe a person's job:

- *She's an accountant.*

You use **a/an** in prices, speeds, etc:

- *$100 a day*
- *50 cents a pack*
- *70 kilometres an hour*
- *three times a week*

No article

You do not use an article when you are talking in general:

- *I love flowers (all flowers).*
- *Honey is sweet (all honey).*
- *Lawyers are well paid (lawyers in general).*

You *do not* use **the** with most names of countries, counties, states, streets, or lakes:

- *I'm going to Turkey.*
- *a house in Walton Street*
- *She's from Yorkshire.*
- *Lake Louise*
- *They live in Iowa.*

or with a person's title when the name is mentioned:

- *President Kennedy*
   BUT *the President of the United States*

Possessive forms

You can add **'s** to a word or a name to show possession. It is most often used with words for people, countries and animals:

- *Ann's job*
- *the children's clothes*
- *the manager's secretary*
- *the dog's basket*
- *my brother's computer*
- *Spain's beaches*

When the word already ends in a plural **s**, you add an apostrophe after it:

- *the boys' rooms*
- *the Smiths' house*

The possessive adjectives are **my, your, his, her, its, our, your, their**. The possessive pronouns are **mine, yours, his, hers, ours, yours, theirs**. The possessive question word is **whose**.

You use possessive pronouns when you do not need to repeat a noun:

My book is here. Where's yours?

Quantity

Much is used with **uncountable nouns**, usually in negative sentences and questions:

- *I haven't got much money left.*
- *Did you watch much television?*

Much is very formal in affirmative sentences:

- *There will be much discussion before a decision is made.*

Many is used with **countable nouns**, usually in negative sentences and questions:

- *There aren't many tourists here in December.*
- *Are there many opportunities for young people?*

In affirmative sentences, it is more formal than **a lot of**:

- *Many people prefer to stay at home.*

A lot of or (*informal*) **lots of** is used with countable and uncountable nouns:

- *A lot of tourists visit the castle.*
- *He's been here lots of times.*
- *I've spent a lot of money.*
- *You need lots of patience to make model aircraft.*

A little is used with **uncountable nouns**:

- *Add a little salt.*

A few is used with **countable nouns**:

- *I've got a few letters to write.*

Note that in these sentences, the meaning is positive. **Few** and **little** without **a** have a negative meaning.

Grammar Reference

Adjectives

Comparatives and superlatives

To form comparatives and superlatives:

- Adjectives of **one syllable** add **-er, -est**:
cool	cooler	coolest
high	higher	highest

- Adjectives that already end in **-e** only add **-r, -st**:
nice	nicer	nicest

- Some words double the last letter:
wet	wetter	wettest
big	bigger	biggest

- Adjectives of **three syllables** or more take **more, most**:
changeable	more changeable
	most changeable
interesting	more interesting
	most interesting

- Some adjectives of two syllables are like **cool**, especially those that end in **-er**, **-y**, or **-ly**:
clever	cleverer	cleverest

- Words that end in **-y** change it to **-i**:
sunny	sunnier	sunniest
friendly	friendlier	friendliest

- Other adjectives of **two syllables** are like **interesting**:
harmful	more harmful
	most harmful

- Some adjectives have **irregular forms**:
good	better	best
bad	worse	worst

Adjectives with nouns

Most adjectives can be used **before** the noun that they describe or **after** a linking verb:

▸ I need a **new** bike.
▸ This bike isn't **new**.
▸ It's an **interesting** book.
▸ She said the film sounded **interesting**.

Some adjectives **cannot** come **before** a noun. You can say:

▸ Don't wake him – he's **asleep**.
BUT NOT: an asleep child

Some adjectives can **only** be used **before** a noun. You can say:

▸ That was the **chief** disadvantage.
BUT NOT: This disadvantage was chief.

Adverbs

Comparatives and superlatives

The comparative and superlative forms of short adverbs are made with **-er** and **-est**:

fast	faster	fastest

The comparative and superlative forms of most adverbs are made with **more** and **most**:

quickly	more quickly	most quickly

Some common adverbs have irregular comparative and superlative forms:

well	better	best
badly	worse	worst
hard	harder	hardest
little	less	least
much	more	most

Adverbs of frequency

You put adverbs of frequency after **be** and auxiliary verbs, and before other verbs:

- She is **always** on time for lessons.
- He has **never** ridden a horse.

You can put **usually**, **often** and **sometimes** at the beginning or end of a sentence:

- **Usually** I get up at 7am.
- I get up at 7am **usually**.

Prefixes and suffixes

Prefixes

a- not: *atypical*

ante- before: *antenatal* (= before birth)

anti- against: *anti-American, antisocial*

auto- self: *autobiography* (= the story of the writer's own life)

bi- two: *bicycle, bilingual* (= using two languages), *bimonthly* (= twice a month or every two months)

cent-, centi- hundred: *centenary* (= the hundredth anniversary), *centimetre* (= one hundredth of a metre)

circum- around: *circumnavigate* (= sail around)

co- with; together: *co-pilot, coexist, cooperation*

con- with; together: *context* (= the words or sentences that come before and after a particular word or sentence)

contra- against; opposite: *contradict* (= say the opposite)

counter- against; opposite: *counterrevolution, counterproductive* (= producing the opposite of the desired effect)

de- taking sth away; the opposite: *defrost* (= removing the layers of ice from a fridge, etc.), *decentralize*

deca- ten: *decathlon* (= a competition involving ten different sports)

deci- one tenth: *decilitre*

dis- reverse or opposite: *displeasure, disembark, discomfort*

e- using electronic communication: *e-commerce*

ex- former: *ex-wife, ex-president*

extra- 1 very; more than usual: *extra-thin, extra-special* 2 outside; beyond: *extraordinary, extraterrestrial* (= coming from somewhere beyond the earth)

fore- 1 before; in advance: *foreword* (= at the beginning of a book) 2 front: *foreground* (= the front part of a picture), *forehead*

hexa- six: *hexagon* (= a shape with six sides)

in- il-, im-, ir- not: *incorrect, invalid, illegal, illegible, immoral, impatient, impossible, irregular, irrelevant*

inter- between; from one to another: *international, interracial*

kilo- thousand: *kilogram, kilowatt*

maxi- most; very large: *maximum*

mega- million; very large: *megabyte, megabucks* (= a lot of money)

micro- very small: *microchip*

mid- in the middle of: *mid-afternoon, mid-air*

milli- thousandth: *millisecond, millimetre*

mini- small: *miniskirt, mini-series*

mis- bad or wrong; not: *misbehave, miscalculate, misunderstand*

mono- one; single: *monolingual* (= using one language), *monorail*

multi- many: *multinational* (= involving many countries)

non- not: *non-alcoholic, nonsense, non-smoker, non-stop*

nona- nine: *nonagon* (= a shape with nine sides)

octa- eight: *octagon* (= a shape with eight sides)

out- more; to a greater degree: *outdo, outrun* (= run faster or better than sb)

over- more than normal; too much: *overeat, oversleep* (= sleep too long)

penta- five: *pentagon* (= a shape with five sides), *pentathlon* (= a competition involving five different sports)

post- after: *post-war*

pre- before: *prepay, preview*

pro- for; in favour of: *pro-democracy, pro-hunting*

quad- four: *quadruple* (= multiply by four),

Grammar Reference

quadruplet (= one of four babies born at the same time)
re- again: *rewrite*, *rebuild*
self- of, to or by yourself: *self-taught*
semi- half: *semicircle*, *semiconscious*
septa- seven: *septagon* (= a shape with seven sides)
sub- 1 below; less than: *subzero* 2 under: *subway*, *subtitles* (= translations under the pictures of a film)
super- extremely; more than: *superhuman* (= having greater power than humans normally have), *supersonic* (= faster than the speed of sound)
tele- far; over a long distance: *telecommunications*, *telephoto lens*
trans- across; through: *transatlantic*, *transcontinental*
tri- three: *triangle*, *tricycle*
ultra- extremely; beyond a certain limit: *ultramodern*
un- not; opposite; taking sth away: *uncertain*, *uncomfortable*, *unsure*, *undo*, *undress*
under- not enough: *undercooked*
uni- one; single: *uniform* (= having the same form)
vice- the second most important: *vice-president*

Suffixes

-able, -ible, -ble (to make adjectives) possible to: *acceptable*, *noticeable*, *convertible*, *divisible* (= possible to divide), *irresistible* (= that you cannot resist)
-age (to make nouns) a process or state: *storage*, *shortage*
-al (to make adjectives) connected with: *experimental*, *accidental*, *environmental*
-ance, -ence, -ancy, -ency (to make nouns) an action, process or state: *appearance*, *performance*, *existence*, *intelligence*, *pregnancy*, *efficiency*
-ant, -ent (to make nouns) a person who does sth: *assistant*, *immigrant*, *student*
-ation (to make nouns) a state or an action: *examination*, *imagination*, *organization*
-ed (to make adjectives) having a particular state or quality: *bored*, *patterned*
-ee (to make nouns) a person to whom sth is done: *employee* (= sb who is employed), *trainee* (= sb who is being trained)
-en (to make verbs) to give sth a particular quality; to make sth more ~: *shorten*, *widen*, *blacken*, *sharpen*, *loosen*, (but note: *lengthen*)
-er (to make nouns) a person who does sth: *rider*, *painter*, *banker*, *driver*, *teacher*

-ese (to make adjectives) from a place: *Japanese*, *Chinese*, *Viennese*
-ess (to make nouns) a woman who does sth as a job: *waitress*, *actress*
-ful (to make adjectives) having a particular quality: *helpful*, *useful*, *beautiful*
-hood (to make nouns) 1 a state, often during a particular period of time: *childhood*, *motherhood* 2 a group with sth in common: *sisterhood*, *neighbourhood*
-ian (to make nouns) a person who does sth as a job or hobby: *historian*, *comedian*, *politician*
-ical (to make adjectives from nouns ending in -y or -ics) connected with: *economical*, *mathematical*, *physical*
-ify (to make verbs) to produce a state or quality: *beautify*, *simplify*, *purify*
-ing (to make adjectives) producing a particular state or effect: *interesting*
-ish (to make adjectives) 1 describing nationality or language: *English*, *Swedish*, *Polish* 2 like sth: *babyish*, *foolish* 3 fairly; sort of: *longish*, *youngish*, *brownish*
-ist (to make nouns) 1 a person who has studied sth or does sth as a job: *artist*, *scientist*, *economist* 2 a person who believes in sth or belongs to a particular group: *capitalist*, *pacifist*, *feminist*
-ion (to make nouns) a state or process: *action*, *connection*, *exhibition*
-ive (to make adjectives) having a particular quality: *attractive*, *effective*
-ize, -ise (to make verbs) producing a particular state: *magnetize*, *standardize*, *modernize*, *generalize*
-less (to make adjectives) not having sth: *hopeless*, *friendless*
-like (to make adjectives) similar to: *childlike*
-ly (to make adverbs) in a particular way: *badly*, *beautifully*, *completely*
-ment (to make nouns) a state, an action or a quality: *development*, *arrangement*, *excitement*, *achievement*
-ness (to make nouns) a state or quality: *kindness*, *happiness*, *weakness*
-ology (to make nouns) the study of a subject: *biology*, *psychology*, *zoology*
-or (to make nouns) a person who does sth, often as a job: *actor*, *conductor*, *sailor*
-ous (to make adjectives) having a particular quality: *dangerous*, *religious*, *ambitious*
-ship (to make nouns) showing status: *friendship*, *membership*, *citizenship*
-ward, -wards (to make adverbs) in a particular direction: *backward*, *upwards*

-wise (to make adverbs) in a particular way: *clockwise*, *edgewise*
-y (to make adjectives) having the quality of the thing mentioned: *cloudy*, *rainy*, *fatty*, *thirsty*

OXFORD
UNIVERSITY PRESS

Great Clarendon Street, Oxford OX2 6DP

Oxford University Press is a department of the University of Oxford.
It furthers the University's objective of excellence in research, scholarship,
and education by publishing worldwide in

Oxford New York

Auckland Cape Town Dar es Salaam Hong Kong Karachi
Kuala Lumpur Madrid Melbourne Mexico City Nairobi
New Delhi Shanghai Taipei Toronto

With offices in

Argentina Austria Brazil Chile Czech Republic France Greece
Guatemala Hungary Italy Japan Poland Portugal Singapore
South Korea Switzerland Thailand Turkey Ukraine Vietnam

OXFORD and OXFORD ENGLISH are registered trade marks of
Oxford University Press in the UK and in certain other countries

© Oxford University Press 2010

The moral rights of the author have been asserted

Database right Oxford University Press (maker)

First published 2010
2014
10 9 8 7

No unauthorized photocopying

All rights reserved. No part of this publication may be reproduced,
stored in a retrieval system, or transmitted, in any form or by any means,
without the prior permission in writing of Oxford University Press,
or as expressly permitted by law, or under terms agreed with the appropriate
reprographics rights organization. Enquiries concerning reproduction
outside the scope of the above should be sent to the ELT Rights Department,
Oxford University Press, at the address above

You must not circulate this book in any other binding or cover
and you must impose this same condition on any acquirer

Any websites referred to in this publication are in the public domain and
their addresses are provided by Oxford University Press for information only.
Oxford University Press disclaims any responsibility for the content

ISBN: 978 0 19 481728 8

Printed in China

This book is printed on paper from certified and well-managed sources.

ACKNOWLEDGEMENTS

Illustrations by: Janette Bornmarker: pp.13, 107; Tim Bradford: pp.25, 38, 60; Mark Duffin: pp.64, 69 (weather symbols); Sally Elford: pp: 16, 35, 83, 85, 93; Joy Gosney: pp.11, 14, 20, 22, 62, 80, 97; Tim Marrs: pp.10, 17, 57, 67, 77; Wille Ryan: pp.49, 68, 70, 82, 99; Myles Talbot: pp.66, 90.

Licensed Illustrations by: Julia Barber/New Division p.36; Jan Bowman p.30; Tim Bradford/Illustrationweb.com pp.29, 52, 75 (sailor etc), 87, 95; Erica Burns/Illustrationweb.com pp.18, 78, 79; Jessie Ford/CIA pp.81, 108; Chris Garbutt/Arenaworks.com pp.72, 91, 101; Peter Mac pp.26, 58, 75 (create), 96; Glen McBeth pp.21, 34, 44, 109; MCKIBILLO pp.62 (face), 65, 100; Clare Rollet/Illustrationweb.com pp.55, 89; Robert Shadbolt p.47 (watch); Magic Torch p.69 (barometer); Carole Verbyst/NB Illustration p.41; Neil Webb/Debutart pp.23, 47 (racing car), 105.

We would like to thank the following for permission to reproduce photographs: Alamy pp.9 (C/Eric Nathan), 15 (Art Kowalsky), 19 (C/Dave Stamboulis), 20 (B/Nigel Pavitt/John Warburton-Lee Photography), 23 (B/i4images - premium), 25 (Mario and Lucia/40260.com), 34 (D/Alex Segre), 37 (archaeology/Tony Kwan), 37 (Brussels arcade/Ian Dagnall), 44 (Fabrice Bettex), 48 (3/Ghislain and Marie David de Lossy/Cultura), 50 (A/Jeff Greenberg/Robert Harding Picture Library Ltd), 50 (B/Steven Ainsworth/Stock Connection Blue), 50 (C/Chris Pancewicz), 50 (D/Petr Svarc), 50 (E/geordiepics), 51 (Doug Hall), 52 (Lisa/Tetra Images), 52 (Henri and Isabelle/Tetra Images), 52 (Pieter and Dagmar/Radius Images), 61 (1/Peter M. Wilson), 78 (Paula and Sally/Redchopsticks.com), 84 (A/blickwinkel), 85 (plastic ducks (top)/Keith Leighton), 92 (Tim Hill), 102 (6/Chris Rout), 104 (GoGo Images Corporation); Corbis pp.16 (2/Jose Luis Pelaez, Inc.), 18 (A/Paul Seheult/Eye Ubiquitous), 19 (B/Redlink), 20 (D/Michael Reusse/Westend61), 24 (A/moodboard), 24 (D/Randy Faris), 24 (E/Lawrence Manning), 25 (Olivia/Phillip Graybill), 27 (Lee Frost/Robert Harding World Imagery), 28 (1/Michael Haegele), 28 (2/moodboard), 32 (ImageShop), 34 (B/Tim Pannell), 37 (chocolate/Neil Emmerson/Robert Harding World Imager), 48 (4/Corbis Yellow), 52 (Jamie and Antoinette/Bernd Vogel), 54 (B/Destinations), 60 (Fernando Alvarado/EPA), 74 (A/Image Source), 76 (Lucy/moodboard), 76 (Joe/Radius Images), 76 (Luke/Ale Ventura/PhotoAlto), 78 (Jessica and Helen/Annie Engel), 78 (Lucas and Linda/Josef Lindau), 84 (D/John Miller/Robert Harding World Imagery); Getty Images pp.9 (A/Paul Harris), 9 (B/Peter Adams), 16 (1/Jochen Sand), 18 (B/Christopher Groenhout/Lonely Planet Images), 18 (C/Darryl Leniuk/The Image Bank), 19 (D/Paul Chesley/National Geographic), 19 (C/John & Lisa Merrill/Stone), 20 (G/Erik Simonsen/Photographer's Choice), 20 (C/B.Schmid/amana Images), 20 (F/Kin Images/Digital Vision), 20 (A/Richard Leeney/Dorling Kindersley), 24 (B/O. Louis Mazzatenta/National Geographic), 24 (C/Stephen Oliver/Dorling Kindersley), 25 (Michael/Marc Debnam/Stone), 33 (Michael Kappeler/AFP), 34 (E/Oli Scarff), 39 (break dancer/John Lamb/Stone), 39 (glass roof/Frederic Cirou/PhotoAlto), 39 (Alain Robert/Carlos Alvarez), 40 (rich dog/Plush Studios/Blend Images), 40 (cat wedding/Meredith Parmelee/Stone), 41 (1/Meredith Parmelee/Stone), 41 (2/altrendo images), 43 (wolf and moon/Francesco Reginato/Stone), 45 (Chris Jackson), 48 (2/Rich Reid/National Geographic), 48 (5/Cameron Spencer/Digital Vision), 54 (A/Chad Ehlers), 59 (illuminated trees/Scott Barbour), 61 (2/Giuseppe Cacace), 63 (Hayley Madden/Redferns), 74 (B/Frank and Helena/Cultura), 76 (Mary/Darrin Klimek/Photodisc), 76 (Mark/Siri Stafford/Riser), 76 (Susan/Andreas Brandt/Lifesize), 76 (Jane/Image Source), 76 (David/Brad Wilson/Photographer's Choice), 78 (Matt/AAGAMIA/Stone), 78 (Ben and Kim/Glow Images), 86 (Great Barrier Reef/Grant V. Faint/Iconica), 88 (B/Dev Carr/Cultura), 98 (DreamPictures/The Image Bank), 102 (3/PNC/Photographer's Choice RF), 102 (1/Brooke Slezak/The Image Bank), 102 (4/Yellow Dog Productions/The Image Bank), 102 (2/Comstock), 106 (A/Bambu Productions/Iconica), 106 (B/Jetta Productions/Lifesize); The Ronald Grant Archive p.43 (The Wolf Man/Universal Pictures); The Kobal Collection pp.42 (A/Dreamworks), 42 (B/Pathe Pictures Ltd), 42 (C/Warner Bros/DC Comics), 42 (D/Paramount), 42 (E/Paramount), 42 (F/GK Films); Mirrorpix p.59 (Duncan Hamilton with iron); Photolibrary.com p.23 (C/David Clapp/Oxford Scientific (OSF)), 23 (D/Colin Monteath/Oxford Scientific (OSF)), 23 (E/Hans Petersen/Photononstop), 25 (Kaito/panoramaMedia), 25 (Ella/Fancy), 46 (B/Benelux Benelux/Cusp), 48 (1/Jesco Tscholitsch/Fancy), 52 (Ferdinand/Fancy), 71 (Juergen Stumpe/LOOK-foto), 84 (C/Siepmann), 84 (B/Daniel J. Cox/Oxford Scientific (OSF)), 86 (rhinoceros/K Wothe/Picture Press), 88 (A/MIXA Co. Ltd.), 94 (1/4x5 Coll-Anton Vengo/Superstock), 94 (4/Ariel Skelley/Blend Images RF), 94 (3/White), 102 (5/Hill Street Studios/Blend Images RF); Rex Features pp.20 (E), 23 (A/The Travel Library), 34 (A/Mike Longhurst), 34 (C/Paul Cooper), 46 (A/Neale Haynes), 46 (C/Zena Holloway), 76 (William/OJO Images), 76 (Harry/WestEnd61), 94 (2/Image Source); Stagecoach Theatre pp.12 (rehearsal), 12 (students from Stagecoach Tunbridge Wells perform 'Downtown'/Photo Sam Pearce).

Images supplied by: Suzanne Williams/Pictureresearch.co.uk

Pages 118–127 adapted from Oxford Wordpower 3E © Oxford University Press 2006